Lorell,

I love you girl.

Thanks for your support.

Love Kimmie

9/16/12

THE KALEIDOSCOPE OF KIMETRY

Kimberley Evans-Reed

AuthorHouse™
1663 Liberty Drive
Bloomington, IN 47403
www.authorhouse.com
Phone: 1-800-839-8640

First published by AuthorHouse   07/23/2011

ISBN: 978-1-4634-3337-6 (sc)
ISBN: 978-1-4634-3336-9 (hc)
ISBN: 978-1-4634-3335-2 (ebk)

Library of Congress Control Number: 2011911258

Printed in the United States of America

Face Painting by: Dervelle Harris/Lamar Edwards Exclusive Salon

To James, the love of my life.

Thanks for believing in me and inspiring me to follow my heart & God's plan for my life. Your love, patience, and your kind spirit make every moment with you a true gift from God. Even though I don't tell you often enough, I've grown to need you like the air I breathe, and I look forward to spending the rest of our lives together. You are the type of hubby that most women dream of having & I am blessed to call you my soul mate.

To Janique, Jasmine, Kimari & Jamie.

Thanks for being four of the most incredible blessings of my life. You all have always been true inspirations to me. A mother couldn't ask for any better gifts from God then the daughters He's trusted me to raise, love & protect. Remember that next-to-HIM, your mom will always be your best friend.

To Mom, Wolf, Sonya, Cheryl, Joy, Kim, & Yvetta.

Thanks for holding me accountable and pushing me when I didn't feel like being pushed. You all may have pressed my last nerve, but I know it was always with a loving spirit. I will always be grateful for it.

To my Dad – William B. Evans III 6/26/1949 – 8/12/2010.

You stepped up to the plate at 17 years old & took on the responsibility of a 2 month old baby girl that you didn't create. From that moment you were my daddy in every way. That one unselfish act turned into many, more & I will forever be grateful. Remembering the last phone conversation we had on my birthday, August 4, 2010. You held me accountable for not sharing my gift of poetry with the world through publishing. You asked me a question that provoked my thoughts. "What does your poetry mean to you baby-girl?" You told me to write it down & to call you back when I was done. I wrote it, but never got around to reading it until the day of your funeral a week later. I miss you daddy. I hope I've made you proud.

KALEIDOSCOPE
ka·lei·do·scope (kə-lī'də-skōp')

A constantly changing set of colors. A series of changing phases or events, a kaleidoscope of illusions with many changing colors, sights, and impressions.

YOUR PATH IS YOUR OWN

We allow people to pressure us into doing things that really don't represent our true character. We allow people to talk us into believing that our path is what "they" see it to be. We do things to "go-along-with-the-flow" and in the midst of all of that . . . we lose ourselves. Promise yourself that you'll find your calling & live it out the way GOD intended. It's beautiful to know what you were created for.

Photo by Keith Bell/Titan Entertainment

SOW HEARTACHE . . . REAP HEARTACHE

Remembering a time years ago when I acted recklessly & selfishly. Stepped out & left someone's heart torn. With much regret for the way I treated him; I asked for his forgiveness. I accepted responsibility for my actions & promised never to treat another person that way again. It was clear that he wasn't the man for me, but it was even clearer that I would reap exactly what I sowed.

Two years later . . . I reaped it 100 times worse, and I am so grateful that God taught me that lesson. It was one of the most important lessons of my life. He had to show me the pain and heartache I caused. He needed me to know what it felt like, so that I would never inflict that on another person. God wasn't about to bring another good man in my life until I understood what true love does when she's bored.

Thank You Lord God!

SIN

When you make the choice to go against God and sin, it doesn't just affect you. Your sin could have a direct or indirect affect on other people. Often we don't think of the consequences of our sins until it's too late and lives are already disturbed or even destroyed. Although you can apologize, you can never really take back what you've done.

Ask God to help you in the areas where you are most weak. Remember, it's not only for you, but the people you care about as well. This is experience talking.

HIDING

Many of us are still living our lives being afraid to be vulnerable to people . . . especially the people we care about? When will we have the courage to allow others to see us for who we really are?

We are all faking something, for someone, at some point in our lives. Emotional inadequacies can be hidden from anyone, but God, and that's only because HE knows all.

Many times we have been through so much that we build a wall of darkness. We hide behind that wall and create an extension of the person we'd rather other people see instead. Sooner or later that extension grows limbs of its own and suddenly we have no control over the person we've become.

Fear of allowing ourselves to be the person GOD created us to be can cripple many chances of genuine happiness in our lives. Sure, we may seem happy on the outside . . . and we may even feel a sense of happiness for a while. But there is no real joy in living within the shell of your own body if you can not be the person that God created you to be. Stop hiding.

EMOTIONALLY OUTTA CONTROL

We all have those days when we are emotionally out of control & we may not even know the root cause. There are many situations in our lives that are minor when "set-apart", but together—create a big ball of mixed emotions. We can't even put it into words sometimes. We lash out at loved ones & make ourselves believe we are justified in doing so.

Sometimes we need God to show us where we need to make some adjustments. It's not always someone else fault that we feel the way we do. It could very well be that we have problems communicating exactly how we feel to others. We can't expect other people to know what's going on in our heads & in our hearts. They only know either what they see or what they've heard, and even then—their perception of our situation may be totally different then what it really is.

Stop putting expectations on other people that they will never always be able live up too. It's not fair to them, just as it wouldn't be fair to you. When life doesn't seem to be fulfilling your personal needs; going on a rampage and running amok serves no purpose other than making you look totally insane.

It's time for Self-Examination. Get with God & He'll direct your path.

DESTINED TO LIVE & DIE ONCE

If you make the choice to sow judgment & criticism in the lives of other people, you will sooner or later reap the same treatment. The way you live in the earth greatly affects your eternal life.

You're only born once just as you'll only die once. After death you will face judgment. If you're thinking about getting your life right at that point, you'd be a lifetime too late. There is only one chance to live your life according to God's plan, and then . . . what's done is done. There are no do-overs!

You don't have to like this in order for it to be true.
Live well.

LOVE THE HELL OUTTA SOMEBODY

We are never happy about our loved ones repeating the same mistake over & over again. We watch and often never say a word for many reasons. We hesitate confronting them because of the possible negative confrontation that may follow as a result.

It's not always comfortable or easy to tell people what they don't want to hear, but many times it's extremely necessary. Love someone enough to tell them the truth about themselves. They may even reject or you for it, but choosing principle over popularity could very well save them from creating a horrible situation. In the end—they may just thank God for your love & honesty. Either way, do your part.

If we are working towards being true warriors for our Savior, one of the most important assignments is caring enough about another person's "state of mind" to help them get it right.

None of us is or will ever be a perfect people, and we should all be open to receiving instruction as well as delivering it. Having folks in our lives that will hold us accountable in a mature and loving way will prove to be one of the best tools for moving to a higher level in Christ.

Some people will see you as being judgmental, but others will see the maturity and love in what you are really up too. You have to choose what you will allow to encourage and/or discourage your efforts.

I want people to love the hell outta me. I've made the decision to "love the hell outta you. It's your choice to "love the hell outta yourself and to love the hell outta somebody else.

Again, none of us is or will ever be a perfect people. But we are not here to save other people, but to share the good news of the one who does indeed save. Jesus.

WASTED WORRY

Take a moment to think about all the time you've wasted on worrying about the things you cannot see up ahead. Wondering which direction God will be taking your life into next. Going back down memory lane, beating yourself up over the mistakes you've made in the past and wondering how things could have been different had you not made those mistakes?

Now take another moment to ask God to release your past days so that they will not contaminate your future. Let go of how you may or may not have hindered future blessings. God has plenty where those came from and there's nothing you can do about it.

Rest assured that God has never ceased creating and developing the goodness out of your life, and He is using the person you are right now to do it. Whether you decide to give it to Him or not . . . He will always have the glory. Always

STEP UP YOUR GAME

Your appearance can speak volumes about you and you don't even have to open your mouth. Too often most people will make judgments about you before you even say one word. It may not be fair, but it does not make it any less true. We do indeed communicate or mis-communicate to others many different things just by what we are wearing.

While the first impressions are huge, you can also change the impressions you have on people in a positive or negative light. The choice is yours and you should make it count in your favor, especially in a professional atmosphere.

People are impressed by the growth of an individual that they once viewed as someone "not up-to-par." There are tools you can use to enhance the "already" beautiful, talented you. For instance: Books are tools that I will be using to enhance what God has blessed me with already; the love of writing. I love this thing I do, and I continuously shame God by not giving it my best shot at doing it right. I'm praying that I will learn and grow so that I will make Him a proud Father.

We all have some area in our lives where we need to step up our game if we are going to move to the next level. There is no shame in the fact that you need the help; the shame is in being so prideful that you won't reach out and attempt to get it.

Handle your business people.

HAVE YOU EVER?

Have you ever felt as if you were grasping in the dark for whatever is there?

Have you ever found yourself asking God for proof that He hears your cry and will heal the brokenness?

Have you ever stopped to notice just how long you're shopping list of wants and needs have become for GOD?

Have you ever wondered why you tend to harbor old disappointments and why you can't seem to totally let them go?

How many times have you actually grasped gratitude and decided to let GOD know just how grateful you are to HIM?

Have you ever wondered why you tend to become involved with an abundance of meaningless pursuits that are not even worthy of promoting growth?

Have you ever seriously tried to rebuild foundations in certain relationships and wondered why it was even necessary in the first place?

Have you ever been a "people" filler, but still felt an emptiness that was extremely hard to explain to anyone but GOD?

You are not alone.

LIVING IN THE PAST

Living in the past will keep you from moving into the blessings that are ahead. The enemy knows exactly what your insecurities are and he makes it his business to side track every attempt you make to move past the pain of disappointments. He sets road blocks in many forms to keep you discouraged and doubtful about your ability to move to the next level.

Many of us have had those times in our lives when we've been knocked down and broken by different situations. The good news is that we don't have to stay down and we definitely don't have to stay broken. No matter what you've gone through, God makes a way for you to enjoy a new beginning. You have to be willing to step into it. Are you?

WATCH YOUR MOUTH! UGH!

Cutting the edge off of your tongue may prove to be one of your biggest accomplishments. Too many times you've allowed anger to impair your judgment, which caused you to spit harmful words to someone you care about. What makes you believe that being non-negotiable is a character trait that others have to accept? You can be dismissed just like anyone else so get over yourself.

Taking baby steps in the right direction can actually produce adult step results sooner or later. But wouldn't you rather take small adult steps instead? Nothings wrong with shortening your path to grown-up-ville.

If you're always presenting yourself as angry, unforgiving, disappointed, wounded, or bitter, it will immensely affect the way you treat others around you. Although there are people who will pacify you and do their best to lift your spirits, you will also have those who have a low tolerance for your frickin bull & they'll put you in your place.

This is not to disregard or minimize anything that you've gone through. Your hurts, pains and past disappointments are real and you have a right to be affected by your troubles. But at some point you must learn to release the junk that holds you in a state of bondage. It's a matter of a life of bitter emptiness or a life of experiencing real joy. It's your life and it's your choice.

IT CAN BE HARD, BUT YA GOTTA TRY

I know it can be difficult to speak in faith when things are screwed up in your life. I'm no stranger to some of the same past struggles, storms and situations as many other people. However, I've chosen to re-teach myself and re-program my train of thought. I want to be as prepared as I possibly can for what ever storms choose me in the future.

Get hungry for words of encouragement and go after them. Speak words of encouragement so that it feeds the souls and spirits of other people. The positive, faith filled words that come from you are helping to strengthen not only the lives of others, but your own at the same time. It's necessary to get serious about the words you allow to become embedded within your heart and mind.

If God confronted you & told you that everything negative you say from this day forward will come to pass, would you stop & think before you speak? Speak positive words of faith, not negative words of fear! The power of what comes out of your mouth has always been one of the most powerful things in the universe! There will be time when it may be more difficult then others, but it's worth the effort.

LET'S TRY TO FIX IT

2-faced dirty lawyers
Lying media reporters
The greedy politicians
Claiming real religion
Extra marital relations
Overhead vacations
See the writing on the wall
Where's the honor in it all
Sick churches preaching
Fake high school teaching
Nobody's really learning
but everybody's yearning
For love
Judges judging demons
Convicting the rights of free men
And killing off our seed
Tryn to make the world believe
the worst about or people
Here comes the frickn sequel
We're absent
Peep the sly rolling eyes
Why are you surprised?
Pointless talk is cheap
Full of deep deceit
Unisexing hair
It's hard to compare
Adams apple floatn there
Why do you even care
Still a person under there
To be saved
Picture perfect head shot
Til you hear a sudden pop
Brains splattered all around
Body lowered in the ground
Pre-mature blood shed
So much left unsaid
Heavy heart still remains
Confirming valid pain
Love is lost

I BE THE POETRY IN ME

I Be the Poetry in Me
I'd like a little time for me
Some space to release emotional energy
Moments to loosen the choke hold that suffocates me

Time to Glorify the Father with this spiritual gift
So my pen can yell halleluiah as the written Word lifts
His Name

Just a little time to share a piece of me
In an effort to live in my destiny
Creating massive poetry
Celebrating the flow in me
Visualizing the balladry
Trippn' on how it all excites me,
It lives in me,
Begs to escape me,
Warning me,
To let it be exactly what it is to me
It soothes me
It's made for me
And when I create it . . .
Izzzz be every bit of this poetry

The poetic beast eternally
I can dance on this paper, and for a moment I'm free
I can breathe

DELETE

You may not always "want" to, but there are times when you "need" to permanently delete people from your life. Especially when they are far more trouble then they are worth. There is a blessing in being free from toxic miserable people. The beauty of them being gone is that their cruddy behavior is no longer your concern. And remember that they won't take it well either. They will try to smear your name or hurt people you love, but they never really win at all. They only end up bringing themselves down even further. You can not mess with God's Property and expect to be blessed!

HOW YOUR PRAISE AFFECTS OTHERS

People seem to be most affected by your faith when you are wounded, because that's when your testimony has the biggest kick. They notice what your praise looks like when life kicks you in the RUMP! Even if you have to FORCE praise out . . . they just want to know that you do your best to give HIM the GLORY no matter what kind of hell you're in at the moment.

THAT'S WHAT HATER'S DO

Through out your life there will ALWAYS be accusers filing charges against you. There will always be people who will remind you and others about your past. There will be people who are watching & waiting for you to make a mistake. Nothing you do will be good enough for them because they are so hell-bent on you being that old you. The higher you move up, the lower they want you to sink & the harder they'll try to pull you down.

There will always be folks who'll need to tear down your character. They will constantly attempt to put your life under a microscope because it makes them feel just a little bit better about their own crap. They want your life to be as crummy as the one they are living. They have no concept of being happy for others and therefore their mission is to make you as miserable as they are.

Why? I'll tell ya why??? Because that's what Haters do.

SHARING UR BLESSINGS ISN'T BRAGGING, IT'S SHARING UR BLESSINGS

It's a trip when folks are always there for you; listening to all of your struggles and helping you wipe your tears, but as soon as you are happy, & doing swell, those same people have the nerve to say you're bragging!! WTHeck!?

That's when you've gotta get your clip board, check list and a pen, and start deleting names as you see fit.

Stay clear of the FAKERS. They will only speak negative energy into your life.

When you are in your season of blessings you'd better learn to give God the praise for all of it. Don't allow the perception of jealous people to be the cause of you holding back on all praises due to the Lord our God!

ADDICTED TO MY PEACE OF MIND

The old me is finally left behind
I'm addicted to my new peace of mind
Don't want my life to be wasted
Can't turn away, so I'll have to face it
Sad and lonely until I found you
Lost on my own, but this love is true
New life, new birth, I'm born again
Praising You for an eternity with no end

Enemy seeks to destroy all I've found
Threatens to lower me six feet underground
Covering me with the dirt You washed away,
I know that You Lord, have the last say

The old me is left far behind
Addicted to my new peace of mind
Don't want my life to be wasted
Can't turn away, so I'll just face it
Sad and lonely til I found You
Glad I fell in love with You

Oh God, Oh God, Lord of my life,
You are my peace of mind
Keeper of my soul, Lord & light
Only You give me peace of mind
Only You.

FAMILY CAN PLUCK YA NERVE

There will be times when family members will press each and every nerve in your body. There will be arguments that you'll need to win and arguments you'll definitely need to end. When you are tempted to lose your cool and say something hurtful, stop and think. Do yourself a favor and take that opportunity to be the bigger person and walk away. Remove yourself from the entire situation long enough to calm yourself. Once you've said something hurtful you can never take it back. You can always apologize and you may be forgiven, but it may never be forgotten. In some cases, you run the risk of damaging that relationship for many years. It could be the difference between keeping a family united, or maybe losing them for good.

It's our responsibility as family members to do our best to create an atmosphere of peace in our homes. We must create a strong sense of unity and assure that each family member understands what that means.

Remember that it's family and nothing can replace it, but sometimes keeping the peace means letting them go.

IT'S ALL ON YOU

Doubting God doesn't make HIM wrong; it makes you doubt yourself. You can hide behind your doubt, but it doesn't make the word of God any less of the truth.

You can become a powerful testament of God's love, or you can waste the opportunity away. The good news is that He is able to use even the doubtful. You have a choice to be for Him or against Him. His love is available for the taking and He gives it freely. Invite Him in to be the keeper of your heart.

It's all on you.

LET THEM GO!

Stop trying to hold on to people who clearly don't desire to be held! It's not the end of the world although it might feel that way. Time will pass, you will bounce back, and someone else will be smart enough to know when they've got a treasure!! Experience talking . . .

PRAYING ANYWAY

God honors our efforts when we pray for people who have hurt us or done us wrong in any other way.

We know that they will reap what they sow
They will feel the wrath of each & every blow
It's not our job, or our place to make them pay
We are called to love & pray for them anyway
God wants to keep His favor flowing over you
You will also be judged by what you choose to do
So pray for those that have betrayed & hurt you

TRUE FRIEND REMINDERS

A true friend can be trusted with your joys and your pains. They won't betray your trust just because you have a disagreement and/or stop speaking for a while. What's shared as friends—stays right there! That's not only a true friend, but a friend with Remarkable Character.

There is warmness in receiving a card or a letter from a friend for no reason other then to let you know how much they appreciate your friendship.

Friends go above and beyond to make life a little less difficult whenever they can. They shield us at times when we have no idea they are doing it; without seeking recognition or reward.

It's a wonderful thing to know that it's not necessary to talk to friends each and every day; yet still have that bond. Those are many times the best friendships we will ever have the pleasure to experience.

Always treasure those friends that choose to see your inner beauty when the eyes of the world aim at your faults.

Remember that every friendship is different—each has its own purpose in your life. Your true friends will understand that their place can never been taken because each one has its own place in your heart.

TRUE FRIENDS welcome your GOOD SEASONS even as they are in turmoil. They know that celebrating the blessings of others is vital to the blessings flowing in their direction.

One of the best things about having lifelong friendships is the "Remember Whens?" They can turn a regular moment into hours of laughter that makes our faces ache like crazy. When is the last time you had a "Remember When" session? I dare ya to create some happiness!

TRUE FRIENDS—THROUGH THICK & THIN
Me and my 2 oldest daughters.

DON'T BE BLINDED

Don't be blinded by your pride. Don't be blinded by your greed.
Open The Book, then open your heart and plant the seed.
Where there is seed there is hope.
So live in it.

Open your mind, release your pride
Let the pain within your heart be crucified
Hopelessness is not an option
Victory is up for adoption

Grab hold to the Spirit of Healing
Let HIM know what it is you're feeling
Do not continue to fight yourself
God loves you even despite yourself

Don't be blinded by your pride
Don't be blinded by your greed
Open the Book & your heart
Dare to plant the seed.

Kimmie wishes you every—Peace

BEING BOLD ABOUT IT

There are places in the world where our lives and safety would be threatened just for being bold enough to share our faith. Yet we live in a place where the worst that could happen to us is that we might lose a friend, a family member or maybe even a co-worker or two.

Many of us would rather keep our faith in our back pocket instead of share it openly with others. There are folks that you'd never know were faith filled people if they didn't actually tell you.

I'm asking God to give us the hearts to want to speak out about Him with a heart, mind, and tongue of boldness, confidence and love. We owe Him at least that much.

HIS SEX IS SEPARATE FROM HIS LOVE

His sex is easily separated from how he feels about you.
If you can't do the same, stop having sex so casually.
Stop playing yourself dear heart.
Allow love to find you.

IT'S JUST SEX

There's a big difference between working on a relationship and wasting your time. Before you throw yourself into the dead-center of a relationship, make sure the other person knows he/she is actually in it. It's crazy how some folks just assume a night of passion means a commitment. It's just sex! Duh

ACCEPT RESPONSIBILITY

It's your life, it's your choice. You need to accept responsibility and do whatever it takes to earn the trust back, or risk losing the person you love for good. Not being honest with yourself and your partner is a breading ground for more of the same; dishonesty. One lie begets another and then another. Before long, you could have a tree of lies that you are unable to control. Accepting responsibility means being honest & owning up to your betrayal. It also allows your partner to have the choice of whether he/she wants to forgive and continue in the relationship or move on. Either way, at least you'll know that you've done your part.

HEMMED YOU UP

All I can do is talk you through this,
But you've gotta wanna do this
Time to stop crying the blues,
Different clues, but same old news
He made you feel complete somehow
But all you feel is weak right now
His game was pretty-damn good right?
His sex was next to dat Kryptonite
Hemmed you up like a cheap quick weave.
Asking his permission so you could breathe
Kept you wet like seaweed.
Then left you hanging like a sea breeze
Broken-hearted and regretful
Tears departed, yet unforgettable
Pray to the Father, "Help me through this"
He's the Only One that can get you through this

ENEMY TERRITORY

You seem oblivious to your lack of control
And no idea when to hold 'em or fold

Counterfeit affections, because your heart is cold
Suffering rejections, because you're not as bold

Paper chasing for pennies, just to bye a dime
Flying high, new beginnings, running out of time

Abandoned all the good things you were taught
Just a matter of time before you're caught

Confusion consumes every part of your mind
Wishing you could quickly hit the rewind

Trouble seems to follow where ever you go
Puff-Puff, pass-pass, the green vapors flow

Losing God's covering as each day sees night
When will you have sense enough to stop this fight?

You've crossed the line & it's the same sad story
You're walking blind in enemy territory

LASTING RELATIONSHIPS

If you depend on those butterflies to keep your relationship on cloud nine, you'll have a rude awakening. That's just too much responsibility for butterflies.

It's important to create moments when you and your mate can pretend that no one else is on this planet but the two of you.

Showering together can turn water into music.

It's a privilege to have the gift of sex so take care of it.

LETTING YOUR GUARD DOWN

It can be hard to let your guard down after you've been hurt. The moment you're heart-broken many of us decide that no one else will ever be allowed to get that close again. We think we are doing ourselves a favor, when actually we could be missing out on our blessing. You can "be careful" without giving up. It isn't always easy, but it's definitely not worth losing the blessing that GOD is sending your way. Don't build that wall so high that your soul mate can't climb over.

ENJOY THE SEASON UR IN

Ecclesiastes 3:1 says that, "There is a time for everything, and a season for every activity under heaven." We should learn to just enjoy the season we are in, to the best of our ability instead of wasting valuable time worrying about things that haven't or may not even happen. Most of us have been HURT, BETRAYED, DISAPPOINTED, or just PIST in a bad way. But if we allow those things to ruin the good things in our life . . . that's on us.

DIVINE PURPOSE

It's hard to swallow and accept some of the challenges that come our way. Sometimes it's even hard to praise God when we are in the midst of adversity. But in order for God to truly mold us as only He can, we've got to understand that He has a divine purpose for each and every challenge.

We will not always understand He's methods or reasons for allowing certain trials, but it's not always meant for us to understand it. Just know that God's plan is better than any plan we could ever dream up for our lives. All that He allows will always end up working for the good.

HER NEEDS ARE AS IMPORTANT AS HIS

When a women works all day, cooks dinner for her family, helps with homework, irons school clothes and folds laundry, one of the last things she wants to do is to look into her man's face and see SEX written all of over it. Even though she knows that her husband's needs should be a priority, she also knows that her needs should be his priority as well.

There's nothing wrong and everything right with showing the same type of unselfish love that your wife shows you. So take sometime and just rub her feet, pour her a glass of wine and just relax with her. Let her relax on your chest and be your loving caring self by holding her until she falls asleep. More than likely she'll respond in a positive way once she's had some simple rest. Ya never know . . . she just might find that energy in the middle of the night. And if she sleeps the night away, at least you'll know that she's confident in the love and consideration that her man has shown her. Showing her that her needs are as important as yours is pretty darn sexy.

GETTING THE SPARK BACK!
(Love is what you do!)

What can you do when the hustle and bustle of life is allowed to slowly break down your relationship? When your sweetheart seems more like a roommate then your sweetheart? When the sparks have disappeared? When you find yourself possibly checking out other "options" on the outside of the relationship?

We can't help being attracted to other people. We *can* help what we do about it. Be responsible! Don't risk losing a good mate over a few relationship issues. Starting over takes work. It's only fun in the beginning because people always show you their best side first! Those butterflies will disappear with that person too. Love is what you do. Your Commitment is shown when you fight to get the sparks back.

Start by praying for the restoration of your relationship. Seek forgiveness and accept responsibility for your role in the death of the sparks. Forgive any possible offenses against you and you're ready to move forward.

Moving forward may mean letting go of the idea that the relationship is over. Change your mind-set by deciding that today is a new beginning. Even though negative circumstances may have tarnished certain areas within the relationship, you can also change directions by focusing on the positive aspects of one another.

Make the decision to start dating each other again. Every relationship should have date-nights or even date-days, which ever works. Take that special time with one another; and focus on the needs and desires of the other person.

Remember when there was nothing you wouldn't do just to make your sweetheart smile? There was a time when nothing mattered but making your honey happy and providing for their every need. If you didn't know how to make it happen, you made it a priority to learn. This is the ACTION aspect of LOVE.

STOP BELIEVING THAT CLOWN

Stop brain washing yourself into believing that CLOWN is actually sorry. The truth may be that he doesn't want you, but he doesn't want to let you go just yet. That's selfish, not love.

You are not the reason he cheats! It isn't because you're not pretty, sexy, or smart enough. It's not you at all. It's the fact that he is a greedy, selfish, inconsiderate fool who is more-than-likely trying to conquer as much BOOTAAHHH as he can before the day he dies!

WTH!?!

Where in the hell was your protection?!
Did either of you even make the suggestion?!
Were you so caught up in his affection?
Did you even think about possible conception?!

Hell yeah, I'm being sarcastic!
Where in the hell was the prophylactic?!
This is plain and simple mathematics
And don't accuse me of being too dramatic!
This isn't a time to be melodramic;
I'm pist off and I'm bringing the static!
I don't give a sh_t about his charismatic!
I don't give a sh_t about his acrobatics!
The SEX process should be systematic!
If you're gonna do-it, bring the plastic!

What does it take for your brain to activate?!
Condom first fool and THEN ejaculate!
There are books that even illustrate!
There are books that even demonstrate!
It takes one moment to hesitate!
Be responsible before you penetrate!

This is easy crap to regulate!
Yet so many people under estimate!
They percolate and procreate
Then spend the money to terminate!

These words are not meant to humiliate,
And I really feel that it's right to reiterate!
You should take the time to communicate
Before you decide to penetrate!
UGH!

TOTAL CHAOS

Fake Christians lying
Children still dying
What are we here for?
Shouldn't we expect more?

Masters of deception,
Claiming their perfection,
Their major contribution
Is serving persecution

Constant chaos & destruction
Minds on mental abductions
Trick justified obstructions
Repeating evil introductions

Every sin participates
Rushes in to regulate
Sucks you under & segregates
Steals your life & seals your fate

Total Chaos . . .

VIP'S OF MASS CONFUSION

Walking Illusions—
VIP's of Mass confusion—
These are some of the people that we call friendzzz.
Be mindful of who you're chosen

It's time to fight for so much more
What are you just sitting there for?
Why do you complain about your situation?
Yet linger in fearful hesitation
Freedom aint coming to knock on your door
Chairs pushed back and feet to the floor
No masquerading for goodness sake
It's warfare and this is give and take

Let go of that victim mentality
Heave the words of this poetry
Stop excepting the same sick illusions
Step away from that same sick confusion
Delete the VIP's of mass confusion
Now tell me who you should be chosen?

TRAPPED

Greed has you blinded
Pride has you warp-minded
Masquerading like a superstar
Fake-parading battle-scars

You don't realize, your mind's infected
Trapped inside, you stand erected
Frozen prize, and anyone gets it
All tongue tied, and can't correct it

You must decide, how you'll end it
Uncircumcised & you can't resend it
Lost your stride & won't believe it
Nowhere to hide & karma sees it

Maintaining lies & sounding twisted
To your demise, the fog's been lifted
With open eyes, all are shifted
Repent or fry, the curse can be lifted

YOU'RE NOT THE BOSS-OF-ME!

Things can get really bad when both people in the relationship are engaged in a constant power struggle over one another. It's as if they've forgotten that each one of them came into the relationship with their own set of thoughts & ideas etc. A relationship can be filled with a bunch of wonderful things and yet still be a relationship that's unhealthy.

Sometimes we get so comfortable with one another & we forget that a relationship is about give-and-take. It's important that both people make compromises and be honest about how you're feeling. We are never going to always agree and/or like everything our partner does. That's what makes the union interesting.

GET READY

God is the one who plants the seed of a dream in our lives. He creates the vision and He wants us to be excited about it. But it's our responsibility to be alert to those opportunities. It's our responsibility to be prepared to take advantage of them and to meet each challenge head-on. When opportunities knock, you need to be ready to seize them.

You can be the best prepared for opportunities when you know who you are. Many of us spend so much time pretending to be something or someone we are not, which hinders our chances of taking full advantage of the blessings presented to us.

Get ready.

VICTIMIZER OR VICTIM?

Victimizer or Victim? I've made a choice to be neither.

DEAD TONGUE

Your dead fruit, *seems deeply rooted*
Your empty words are heavily diluted

Constant destruction flows from your tongue
Nothing positive to teach your number one

Obsessed with those who can't stand you.
Exiled by most of your own family crew too

Caught up in your crazy minded emotions
Begging each lover for undying devotion

Writing a million checks that you can't cash
Now we see you under a magnifying glass

Afraid we're gonna put your crap on blast
Sitting home nervous, puff-puff pass

Your dead fruit, *seems deeply rooted*
Your empty words are *still* heavily diluted

There are a million things you think you know
Wonder if ya knew—you'd reap what you sow

BITTERNESS

Bitterness can become a beast that will devour you if allowed. We all have had unfair and unjust things happen to us, that's just a part of life. When we are hurt, we can either be stubborn and hold on to that pain and become bitter, or we can do our very best to let it go and trust God to make it up to us the way He chooses to.

Learn to rise above the situation and allow our Father God to control the things you can not. Or you can choose to harbor pain and anger and poison your life. You can allow bitterness to burn through you like acid or you can choose to be guided by the Holy Spirit.

Be well.

WHAT YOU WON'T DO . . .
Someone else will.

Some of us get so caught up in our nice & secure relationships that we take our mates for granted. We become selfish, prideful, judgmental, and so many other unpleasant things. We expect our mates to look past our behavior on the basis that they love us; and many times they do look past & they forgive. They forgive us for being stingy with the "goods", and not tending to the needs that we once viewed as high priority.

Forgiveness doesn't mean the need to be loved, appreciated and desire just disappeared. Forgiveness is one of the many ways they show us that their love is unconditional. It shows that their love for us is not based on the mere fact that we never disappoint them. Forgiveness is given freely and out of love . . . . and that's real love.

So, unless you want to witness someone else cherishing the love that was once your own; get it popping.

Just keeping it real.

ALL HURT-UP

She hurt you to your very core
Reached in with her bare hand
Ripped your heart out & left you torn
Left you feeling broken and scorned
Got cho wishing you'd never been born

Never thought it would happen to you
Watching your tear drops reproduce
Played the fool & the tricks played you
Pain ain't the same when it's filling you

Instead of your own trickery and lies
Ya get to see hurt through your own eyes
Ya get to ask all the When? What? & Whyss?
Ya get to miss those hips and thighsssss
Ya get to see her with that other guy
Ya get to hold back on the tears you cry
Ya get to reminisce on the good ole times
Ya get to be ignored while you vocalize
Ya get to OVER DRAMATIZE

DO SOMETHING ABOUT IT!

Why do you complain?
Yet still stay the same.
If your heart remains in pain,
WTH have you really gained?
Repeating the same mistakes,
facing another heartbreak
Giving away your milkshake,
How much more will you take?
Again you're playing the loser
Under the curse of a user
It's time for a rebirth
You've gotta learn your worth
Step away from the worst
Fulfill your destiny on earth
Complete a life transfusion
Pray away the confusion
Summit to the solution
Not a repeated illusion

IT'S WORTH THE PAIN

Totally freaked out by the crazy situation
Question marks of miscommunication
This didn't fit your perfect equation
Yearning for that quick retaliation

Though you've been given confirmation
Your eyes crave their own observation
Butterflies fill your gut with anticipation
As you launch your personal investigation

This is a level of determination
Ignited by hurtful humiliation
In your mind you see the justification
So you hop right in your transportation

All alone you're having a conversation
Knowing there's no satisfying explanation
Then you come to the realization
That he/she ain't worth the damn frustration

You turn around and go home
You go into your room alone
You cry and you pray
You give it all away
TO GOD.

Soon you realize that the entire experience was one of the best stormy lessons of your life.
You realize that sometimes God has to allow you to experience heartbreak just so you'll know how special the blessing will be when it comes.
PRAISE HIM!!

IF IT AIN'T YOURS . . . DON'T TOUCH IT

Stop blaming other people and just face it
It wasn't yours, yet you had to taste it
You didn't think about all the consequences
Made yourself believe your own false pretenses
Dug the wrong hole, and fell head over heels
Creeping in another man's household could've gotten you killed

Failed to put cho crap on pause
Broken a million marital laws
Still trying to excuse your flaws
Feeling like you're breathing thru coffee straws

You should've thought with your other head
Lost your heart in a married woman's bed
Pierced your heart like a needles thread
Slam dunked by the super-head

Stop blaming other people and finally face it
If it don't belong to you; don't frickn taste it

ONE OF THE SEXIEST THINGS ABOUT A MAN

A man that understands that his woman wants to be able to show him affection without it always having to lead to sex is extremely sexy. Knowing how important it is to have an emotional connection with her will enhance your relationship. Sex is a priority to men; women have known this for many moons. But, a man that understands the importance of a woman's need to feel that special closeness without it moving into a sexual nature is absolutely, positively one of the sexiest things about that man to his woman. So if you find yourselves in a season of disconnection . . . this just might be a short, but HUGE piece of information.

RELATIONSHIP REVIVAL

Sacrifices will determine survival
Relationship in need of a revival

First comes needed recognition
Then comes needed intervention

Your keys won't start the ignition
If they're not in the right position

And hearts can't be reconditioned
Without the right ammunition

Time for life-landmark decisions
Under the Highest supervision

Dismiss the blame and criticism
Resist all things that cause division

Surrendering mind, body and soul
Breaking free from all strongholds

COMING OFF OF YOU

Coming off of you,
Is like trying to be caffeine free
What am I to do?
Now that you are absentee?

Please excuse my expression,
I must make this confession
You've been my one obsession
My second-hand smoke detection

Candle lights showing our reflections
Twisted in every direction
I'm missing that special connection
Closes thing to pure perfection

Now I'm paying the full price
Of a foolish chic's paradise
I know that I should think twice
As I feen for sugar and spice

Coming off of you
Is like trying to be caffeine free
What am I to do?
Now that you are absentee?

SHE'Z CRAZY?

NAW mannn! She ain't crazy! That's the 1st thing a loser wants to say when he gets caught! She ain't crazy . . . she's hurt & possibly angry as hell over your betrayal! Stop using that COP-OUT line and take responsibility for your crap! Saying she's crazy doesn't change what you did and it's doesn't keep her from going upside your damn head!

Going upside your head AIN'T right, but it doesn't make her CRAZY! It could get her a charge doe.

OH yeah . . . The thing that makes her crazy is GETTING BACK with your cheating tale.

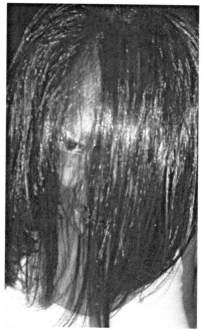

She Ain't Crazy. Is she?

BETRAYED & BROKEN

Voice of a love token
Cracked and heartbroken
Utterly destroyed
Off guard and paranoid
Gave up your "double-jointed
Just to be disappointed
Oh voice of a love token
Sadly misspoken

MARRIED TOO SOON

Cheated once, cheated twice
Cheated while I was his wife
And nothing came easier to me
Then cheating on the man that cheated on me

I had to fuss, I hate to fight
For him to stay home at night
And nothing that this man could say
Would change when I got fed up one day

We were both 21, which was too damn young
Rebelling against parents, immature & dumb

Hardly praying at all; and barely going to church
Thought we did, but didn't know our worth

Racking up debt & messing up our credit
Not giving a crap; we were really pathetic

Bringing babies into this crazy situation
This meant 18 years of a support obligation

Married too soon so it fell like dominoes
Sun turn to gloom so we lost the rainbow

Cheated once, cheated twice
Cheated while I was his wife
And nothing came easier to me
Then cheating on the man that cheated on me

SIX MINUTES?

We collided because we were both misguided
Every trust broken; never should've confided
All was destroyed, everything null and void
We were a picture-perfect, yet a fake Polaroid.

Unevenly yoked, from the first back stroke
Had to give it a laugh, even that was a joke
Six minutes of fun, then he loses control
Should've never let him into my sugar bowl

But that's on me; I shouldn't have been sugar-free
It was "my" body and "my" responsibility
It's not like he just forced me to give it away
Smelled good, talked right & I said "Heeeyy"

What a waste of energy; a total waste of time
All of that great foreplay led to a half-a-grind
You talked a big game, but ended up lame
Moaning & groaning like you were in pain

Really man . . . Is it really that serious?
I'm rolling my eyes, thinking "this is ridiculous"
Six minutes of fun and I'm feeling cheated
While this lame joker is clearly over-heated

Ugh!

BAMMAH DISQUALIFIED!!!

Never imagined dark, dire things
U've jeopardized your family theme,
and the symbol of the wedding rings

Total destruction of marital vows
All eyes are on you now
Feel free to take your bow

Neglecting parental responsibilities
Still claiming your masculinity
Kids calling you "Daddy Houdini"

Habitual liar, and a total misfit
Dramatizer, with no job to quit
Parental guidance, proven unfit

Every promise that you submit
Coming back stamped "counterfeit"
Characteristics of a sad statistic

Prayers lifted for ya kids and x-wife
God blessed them with a Shining Knight
Stepped up to the plate; side by side
You've just been smoked & disqualified

LOOK AT GOD!

HE'S A COWARD!!

HE'S A COWARD and he has you thinking that you're stuck there
You've convinced yourself that he actually really does care
You never thought he could get that angry before,
Until you struggled to pick yourself up from the floor
You're looking into the mirror, yet you still refuse to admit it
It's easier to make excuses for him and you continue to dismiss it

He pulls into the drive way and your kids are terrified
Hot plate on the table; and you pray he's satisfied
Throws his plate to the floor and grabs you by your collar
While your kids can do nothing but cry, scream and holler
Watching their daddy beat their mommy strike by strike
Growing up in a home with an abusive parasite

He's drained your bank account & you don't have a dime
You need to feed your children but your cards are declined
That's another place where you should've drawn the line
Instead you're just looking embarrassed in the checkout line

He's a coward and he knows it
He doesn't love you and he shows it
Balls up his fist and then he throws it
Says he's sorry then he blows it
He's gonna REAP just like he Sows it

PLEASE GET OUT WHILE YOU STILL CAN
Don't lose your life at the hands of this man

FOR THE LAST TIME

I can't live with your love
It's not possible anymore
Every time we argue
You knock me on the floor
Then you make up with your kiss & hugs
Not to mention the tears rolling down your mug

For the last time baby
You've knocked me around
For the last time baby
I can't live with your love

And all the while, the strength that I lacked
Made me forgive and take you back
But now I've finally made up my mind
You've knocked me around for the very last time

For the last time baby
You've knocked me around
For the last time baby
I can't live with your love

BEAT UP

I remember watching different females I cared about get beat on by men. There were several times I could've been seriously injured or actually loss my life. Ya see, I automatically conditioned my brain to immediately make my limbs move and leap into any domestic violence situations when it involved a woman I cared about. Yep, sometimes it was stupid & not the best way to handle it, but in the heat of the moment I just wanted to protect. And it didn't much matter that I didn't have a weapon because I thought I was Wonder Woman. I was more like Might Mouse, but the mission was accomplished either way. Pretty soon one of the "woman beaters" would only come around if I were not in the area. Smile.

I vowed from a very young age that NO man would be allowed to put his hands on me in a harmful way. If he attempted to try his luck . . . I'd have a plan of attack to defend my right to be free from the knuckle prints of his damn fist. Or the finger prints of his hand, or the sole of his shoe.

I've had the pleasure of knocking out a tooth, crushing a set of balls with my mean right grip, landing a blow-to-the-head with a iron cast frying pan, and a few "two-on-one bum-rush jumpers," which included my sister Sonya. GIRL POWER!

The message here is not a message of extended violence, or to send women out to get revenge. The message is to let other women know that these men are only human. They are not indestructible and they are NOT above the law. Defend yourself when necessary and report that dude as soon as possible.

It's not always going to be easy, but this is "your" life and you have a right to live it without physical, mental or emotional abuse.

Be well.

RAPED

Battered and raped
Fought to escape
Duck tied and taped
Burred in the landscape
Trapped underground
Terrified by the sound
Pulled from the danger
Rescued by a stranger
Wouldn't be alive
Without God on his side
This blessed little boy
Could have been destroyed
Cleared hurt & anger from his face
Replaced my Mercy & Grace

INAPPROPRIATELY TOUCHED

It can be hard to trust men when you're a little girl who's been touched inappropriately. Oh come on, let's just say it! He tried to touch me down there when I was sleeping! I was nine years old and he was a grown azz man. I hated him! But I was more ashamed then anything of myself. I hated myself for not remembering what I could have done to make this man that I trusted, try something like that with me?

For the next few years I looked at myself, covered in extra clothes no matter how warm or cold. I covered my rear end because it seemed that was the only body part that was growing at different rate then others. I felt that as long as I covered up just enough, that I could keep anyone from ever wanting to try that again. WRONG! At age thirteen some one else tried it. A friend of a family member, who I thought was a friend to me as well. Guess not.

God was surely on my side since I was saved from what I now know as actual penetration. Although neither of those two fools was successful in actually raping me, they still took something very precious. Trust.

Being afraid and ashamed to mention these acts to anyone caused me to use the only outlet I felt I could always trust. So I picked up a pen and I started to write. Thus, the beginning of what poetry means to me.

I became The Poetic Beast Eternally. I was able to breathe.

HATER-RATION COMPLICATIONS!!

Problematic, psychosomatic
You're a dramatic—fanatic
Causing unnecessary static
I'mma bout to let cho have it!

What's all this hater-ration
Creating complications
Senseless fabrications
With zero confirmation!

If it's any consolation
There waz a brief hesitation
But I felt my obligation,
Was to put these words in rotation

Here's your notification
YOU CAN'T TARNISH my reputation
YOU CAN'T BUY MY sophistication
YOU CAN'T STOP MY acceleration
So just show some appreciation!

Put that hater crap on pause
This battle is UR lost cause
All you got from flapping them jaws,
is the sound of your own applause.

You want my life, but you can't have it
You want my vision, but you can't grab it
Since you intend to create this static
I'mma turn my "PEN dial" on semiautomatic!

If you've got time to hate on me
It's time you've wasted when you could really get to know me

GOSSIP LIER

Mouth on cruise control
Vindictive lies you've told
Major pain choke hold
Unkind empty soul

Never a moment of truth
You and your gossiping troop
Tagging the inside scoop
Never the naked truth

Hasted make waste ya see
Slandering maliciously
Straight face lying to me
Mercy & Grace cover me

YOU FOOL

How dare you chastise,
When you constantly compromise
You all but paralyze,
When you continue to criticize
You pretend not to regonize,
The hearts you jeopardize
Then you ignore the outcries
That put your ego on king size

Looking through snake eyes
You set out to hypnotize
Your wisdom is unwise
No truth when you vocalize
Head on a chopping block
Master of double talk
Claiming brotherhood
Living falsehood
Accused & ridicule
Judged & over ruled

TRAMP

Poison lipstick
Blood sucking tic
Repeated dirty tricks
Back stabbing tramp chics

Common sense busted
Need your brain adjusted
Thief can't be trusted
We're all so disgusted

Talking major chitt
Such a big hypocrite
Living in a snake pit
Parental unfit misfit

Poison lipstick
Blood sucking tic
Twisted point of view
Evil through & through

Back stabbing rejects
Motives always suspect
Over applied cosmetics
You're really so pathetic

Common sense busted
Tramp can't be trusted
We're all so disgusted
Need your mind adjusted

DESPERATE CHICS

Why must you populate the population?
Are you filled with that much desperation?
No hope of wedding invitations,
Yet you insist on procreation

That's just a sadden situation
Creating family with no foundation
Cursing another generation
Another fatherless situation

To HELL with your liberation
This is nothing but manipulation
Creating life with the anticipation
To trap that man in marital relations

That's just sad . . .

WAKE UP MISS SLEEPYHEAD

Your brain must be shipwrecked
You need to have that thing checked
You're giving up your paycheck
To some low-life reject

Wake up Miss Sleepyhead!
Cupid wrote "stupid" on your forehead
You'll never be his newlywed
Only a chic that he takes to bed

I'm looking for your self-esteem
It's laughing at your dumb day dreams
Your hope is running out of steam
Your tank is low on gasoline

I said wake up Miss Sleepyhead!
Don't keep sacrificing your head
See this creep for what he's really worth
Cut him loose and close your purse!

BLIND MAN

Blind man's bluff
Not really rough & tough
Kid & Play handcuffs
Balls of a powder puff
Dishonoring flesh & blood
Character mimics mud
Night life, local clubs
Jail-bait back rubs

Blind man's bluff
Not really rough & tough
Stinky little attitude
Very little gratitude
Populating multitudes
Never buying baby food

Blind man's bluff
Not really rough & tough
Kid & Play hand cuffs
Balls of a powder puff

HATE BURIAL

Why are you still trying to put this woman in a box?
Ain't a box made that can hold what I've got.

Signifying & lying, just trying to bring a sistah down
You're despising—still I'm rising, and going pound for pound

Victimizing & visualizing—hoping for my defeat
Surprised eyes, banged up pride
Wondering how in hell you just got beat

Don't despair—go tie up your hair
You wouldn't wanna sweat out cho perm
Don't be scared—I ain't going no where
Imma preach dis until you learn

Why are still trying to put this woman in a box?
Ain't a box made that can hold what I've got.

What makes you bear that empty fruit?
Why won't you give that bamma the boot?
Instead you'd rather HATE on ME?
Cause I chose to live in VICTORY!
Repent and let your mind be taught
Deception is what you weak mind bought
Next time you'll wanna check your sources
Before running yo lips like chariot horses

No need of trying to put this woman in a box
Your box can't hold nothing I've got

I'm saying a prayer for self control
I'm all about that GIVE AND TAKE
If you decide to keep digging your hole
Try burring some of that senseless HATE.

LITTLE WHITE LIES

Accuser, abuser,
Repeated loser

You pick and choose,
The lives you use

You live and learn,
Out of turn
With no concern
for the hearts you burn

You seem to magnify,
the little white lie
Trying to justify,
why you crucify

Now you've hit a roadblock
Mind blowing mental shock
Heads on the chopping block
Shaken from the aftershock

Still you don't apologize,
All you do is visualize,
the next one you victimize,
gets a new set of little white lies

HATER BLAST!

Staying clear of the drama from the past
No longer feeling the pain of an outcast
Haters standing outside of the looking glass
Pissed cause once again they've been outclassed

They're still waiting to see a stormy forecast
Craving to witness a gloomy overcast
Secretly still talking fake-gossip trash
Jealous of my sexy hourglass

Excuse me if I've made you gasp
I'm putting these haters on major blast
Haters ain't gonna appreciate my backlash
Pen and paper bout to give 'em whiplash

TO BE CONTINUED . . . .

DEM FAKE AZZ PEOPLE 1

Fake azz people
With a million false pretenses
Different levels of hostilities
Many of the same consequences

I'm puttin fake azz people
Out in front so they can face it
To wonder what this really means
You may just need to taste it

Beware of the fake azz people
They prey on your every weakness
Something's always in the making
I need you all to really peep this

Recognize the crummy lies they spreadin
The truth becomes their own deception
Masters in their own minds of minds
The tongue becomes a muscle of infection

Fake azz people or root of the evil
Souls are filled with dark strategy
Hearts of darkness beyond evil
Spirits heavily weighed by gravity

Fake azz people listen up
Change your present condition
War is declared and you can't win
Pray for your own remission

Fake azz people with fake reasons
For the destruction they tend to bring
What's the solution for their pollution?
Why do they love our suffering?

GET A LIFE TERMITE

Your measures are drastic
Your boobies are plastic
Your waist-line is elastic
You need some gymnastic

You've got haters vocabulary
Seems like it's hereditary
Your lies are imaginary
You're extremely unnecessary

You never think twice
Dumb gremlin! Bright Light!
You hate at-any-price
Get a life you termite!

TRIFFLING CHIC

Here's an honorable mention
Back-stabber three dimensions
Giving you needed attention
I'm volunteering intervention

I'm striking back in self-defense
The word-war must now commence
Your lack of simple common sense
Causes suffering at your expense

Nothing you say should be trusted
Your credibility is totally busted
Your sister's heart? You crushed it!
Stole her man, and she's disgusted

Guess what? She did it to you too
You're baby's daddy was her boo
I bet you thought that ish was wack
You dang near had a heart attack

Honestly speaking, you both look crummy
Not just sisters, but two dang dummies

FAKE AZZZ PEOPLE 2

Beware of the fake azz people
They prey on your every weakness
Something's always in the making
I need you all to really peep this

Recognize the crummy lies they spreadin
The truth becomes their own deception
Masters in their own minds of minds
The tongue becomes a muscle of infection

Fake azz people or root of the evil
Souls are filled with dark strategy
Hearts of darkness beyond evil
Spirits heavily weighed by gravity

Fake azz people listen up
Change your present condition
War is declared and you can't win
Pray for your own remission

Fake azz people with fake reasons
For the destruction they tend to bring
What's the solution for their pollution?
Why do they love our suffering?

HATER IN REMISSION

Emotional victim out of control
Digging an even bigger hole
Two-faced lying giants stand
Sucking you in the quicksand
Time for some intervention
Needing a worth-while mission
Devised plan for prevention
This is a hater in remission

TROUBLE MAKER

Full of false pretense
At someone else's expense
Absent common sense
Credibility, one percent

Dramatizing fake events
Can't wait to misrepresent
Each lie came and went
Disguised as a compliment

Your mouth be judgmental
Like reading be fundamental
So if my foot becomes instrumental
It won't be accidental

SHUT UP!

MR. VAPORIZER

Three kids and a possible
Trick ego on colossal
Mind of 21, yet the body on fossil
Claiming to be a religious apostle

Masquerading a human profit
Responsibility, you dropped it
Hiding out, & refused to face it
Time flies, yet still you waste it

Do you even recognize?
Or have the heart to sympathize?
Children are God's butterflies
Yet you make & break their family ties

You're older, but still not wiser
Producing kids like fertilizer
Professional Mr. Vaporizer
Fake bammah apologizer

Your off spring is undeniable
Your word is totally unreliable
Your honor is indescribable
And totally unjustifiable

CARELESS COWARDS—DEADBEAT PARENTS

Careless cowards, creating new population
Your seeds abandoned, in total isolation
Running from your Child Support obligations
Misplaced priorities; fake justifications

Careless cowards, masquerading family ties
Truth be known now, yet still verbalizing lies
Orally fabricating; false fame on the rise
Whole world watching you fantasize

Careless cowards, creating generations
A child's broken heart fills with anticipation
Another year gone by; zero dedication
Oblivious to the moral obligation

Dedicated to Deadbeat Parents Only

DEADBEAT DADDY

I'm not mad because he cheated on me
I ain't even mad that he lied and called me crazy
I'm not concerned that he's always been a momma's boy
It's not my problem he goes through women like old toys
What "does" concern me is that for the past 10 years
He's been a deadbeat daddy, with more than 60K in arrears
The state where I live has a warrant out for his arrest
He works to protect & serve, now ain't that some mess
What kind of man does work that protects others
And won't protect his little girl or her brother
He pretends to catch bad guys to bring them to court
When he's the one running from the office of child support
I'm not even mad that he tried to beat on me
I'm not even mad about that STD
I'm not concerned that he's a trifling male whore
I just thank God I ain't with him anymore
What "does" concern me, is that for the past 10 years
He's been a deadbeat daddy and he doesn't even care

LOST DADDY

I had a dream last night that my daddy came to see me
I opened the door and there he was smiling down at me
He picked me up and gave me a gigantic mega hug
We went to the sand box and made pies out of mud
He reached in his pocket to give me a dollar for an ice cream
cone
Before the dollar touched my hand, I woke up and I was all alone

Mommy says my daddy's lost and he's trying to find his way
I wonder what he's doing now or if he knows it's my birthday
I saved a piece of birthday cake, just in case today's the day
And even if I have to wait I'll ask God to keep him safe when I
pray

My auntie says my daddy's loud, and he's funny just like me
My uncle says he's just a clown, and he knows my daddy loves me
My sister says that he's not lost, and he's hiding behind some wall
Mom told her to say nice things, or don't say anything at all

I had a dream last night that my daddy came to see me
I opened the door and there he was smiling down at me
He picked me up and gave me a gigantic mega hug
We went to the sand box and made pies out of mud

I wonder what he's doing now or if he knows it's my birthday
Another year has gone by and my daddy still hasn't found his way.

AIN'T GOTTA BE NO BABY-MOMMA DRAMA

Every thing waz every-thing while you were bumpin and grinding her
If she said "swing" your ashh would swing & it was all divine to her

The claim of the PILL, is the run of the mill—yeah she sho nuff lied
With your own free will, like Jack & Jill—yo horny tale made that slide

Didn't you even think of the possibility?
Where was the notion of probability?
What made you believe her credibility?
Was it just shear gullibility?
Now comes a new responsibility!

You know you ain't trying to marry her
You sho nuff can't afford to carry her
Things no longer temporary with her
Regretting that missionary with her

You did the deed and you must pay
Planted your seed, & baby's on the way
Stand by the mom & be there for the birth
Experience the best feeling on EARTH

Aint Gotta be No baby momma drama.

I SEE YA

This is for those Husbands/Brothers out here that are truly honoring their commitment of marriage and keeping the family together.

I SEE YA doing you're thing
Honoring the symbol of the wedding ring
Supporting and caring for your offspring
Upgrading your wifey's diamond ring
Turning down opportunities for casual flings
I SEE YA out there doing you're thing

I SEE YA reading stories at bed time
Teaching your babies nursery rhymes
Using GOD's WORD as your life-line
Vowing your love for a life-time
Even when arguments seem like wartime
Ya turning the dial back to peacetime
Apologizing before bed-time

I SEE YA doing ya thing, time-after-time
Never afraid to let you're woman shine
Ignoring how she runs her mouth sometimes
Still letting her know when she's out-of-line
Showing her how she blows your mind
Loving your family til the end of time
I SEE YA

I SEE YA #2

I SEE YA being forced to grieve
Disrespected and deceived
The broken Adam; losing Eve
Aching heart; begging please

I SEE YA tryn to hold the key
Trying to save your family
Praying for the queen bee
"Demon set my woman free"

I SEE YA doing all you can
Trying to be that good man
Gettn' rejected in your homeland
But turning away one-night-stands
Still, you held your woman's hand
And remained her Superman
Pulled her from the quicksand
By seeking the chain-of-command
Prayed for GOD to take her hand
And lead her back to her man

I SEE YA fighting for a chance
Rekindling love and romance
Asking her for a slow dance
Puttn-down that special rain dance

I SEE YA your determination
A good man; an inspiration
Praising GOD with appreciation
HE went above your expectations

I SEE YA leading your family tree
Asking the warrior to intercede
Breaking curses; on bended knees
That's what happens when prayer leads

I SEE YA . . .

I HAD YOU

When my daddy wasn't there to welcome me into the world, I had you
When nightmares frightened my daddy's little girl, I had you
When I came home proudly with a Fathers Day card, I had you
When I got a happy face sticker and three gold stars, I had you
When I fell down outside and scraped my knees, I had you
When I needed the talk about the birds and the bees, I had you
When I went to my high school prom + needed a dress, I had you
When I needed my daddy to get me out of a mess, I had you
When I needed my daddy to walk me down the isle, I had you
When I wanted a limo so I could ride in style, I had you
When life seemed hard to deal with, I had you
When I needed someone I to be real with, I had you
You are my Father and I love you
Thanks for loving me too.

Happy Fathers Day

Dedicated to William B. Evans III, Gregory A. Miller (Wolf) and James R. Reed

SPEAKING IT

We need to speak words of strength, power and encouragement over our lives and the people we love. We bind any negative word that has ever been spoken about or over us, and we place those haters at the feet of God. We bind the spirit of un-forgiveness and the bondage of bitterness. We declare that we are filled with God's supernatural protection at all times. And we believe and declare that God's blessings will forever flow to and through us. We bind the spirit of the orphan and invite the spirit of responsible loving parents for every child.

HEY POP,

You've taught me that a real man isn't afraid to cry
A real man doesn't live his life based on a lie
A real man takes care of his kids
And in a ready-made family he treats them as if they were his
You've taught me that a real man steps up to the plate
He loves even the kids that he didn't create
He provides for his family and respects his wife
And does his best to live a Godly life
So I thank you Pop, for loving and raising me this way
I'm proud to be your KID; & I wish you a Happy Father's Day

STEPPN-UP-2-THE-PLATE!

Her step-dad came into her life when she was 14 years old. She asked "James, do U think I'll get to go to college?" He told her "you make the grades & I'll make sure you get there." Nikki is 24 years old now & graduates next month (May 2009)! This is a prime example of a Step-dad stepping up to the plate. God has each of our steps pre-ordered. This is one of the many blessings that can come to pass if we just walk in those steps.

GLORY-BE-TO-GOD!

BEING A KID

As I remember the special things that made being a kid so awesome, I have to thank God for allowing me to have been so blessed. All of the times momma made a meal out of what ever little we had at the time, while we never realized how hard she had to struggle to do it. The kitchen floors that were so clean we could eat off of them, and we never realized we were living in the ghetto for the entire 3 years we were there. The nice clothes we wore that came from the cheapest store sale racks, and the toys we received from the Salvation Army's Christmas program were things we just didn't think about. Never once did we feel deprived or cheated out of a single thing. For all of this and more, I thank my Lord and Savior—Jesus Christ.

LOLLIPOPS FOR DADDY

Wonder if daddy sees me when I jump, skip and hop
When I get to heaven I'll share my lollipops
Mommy says you're watching me every single day
Daddy is an angel & he protects me in every way
Wonder if daddy sees me when I jump, skip and hop
When I get to heaven, I'll share my lollipops

R.I.P Gregory (Bo) Stone
We miss you.

Velicity

I HATED YOU THEN

Found out about you when I fifteen
Suddenly there's a new daddy on the scene
Didn't want any part of you; I was hurting
Who in the hell was I anymore? I was searching
How could you maintain such a lie?
Had so many questions & I wanted to know why?

Feeling frustrated and devastated,
Humiliated and manipulated
Tears constantly accumulated
Fears rapidly accelerated
Felt like my entire life was suddenly segregated
So many questions kept me so damn aggravated
Was I supposed to love you just because we're related?
Where there gonna be 2 dad's there when I graduated?
It was so hard to take, and far too complicated
All I wanted to do is get intoxicated
I couldn't wait to become totally isolated
To block it all out and become alienated

I wanted the "lie" to be reformulated
Back to when things weren't so complicated
I felt my entire existence had been falsely created
And the truth was damn sure highly over-rated

Everything I knew, had been defaced
My entire family history had been erased
WTH!? Was I just expected to cut-and-paste?!
I couldn't even look you in your damn face!

I felt betrayed, broken & I wanted to die!
Cause I was walking around & living a damn lie!
While you made more babies that you identified
Another man raised me with honor, love & pride
While you neglected me & created a bigger mess
I was the lucky one, to have been so blessed
You didn't even provide child support to take care of me
It was your poor choice to remain absentee.
So why in the HELL did yall have to tell me?!

DARK HEART LIFTED

At first my heart was dark for you
And I didn't wanna be apart of you
You understood and you prayed it through
You knew exactly what God needed to do
You knew that I was taken by surprise
And that one day I would forgive you for the lies
You saw the hurt of my broken condition
You knew this would be a hard transition
As the years went on, you held your ground
You promised to be there and never let me down
We've grown as close as a father and daughter could be
Thank you for finally doing "right" by me.

Dedicated to Gregory D.V. Greene
(dad)

GRAND PA

Grand fathers should never under estimate the impact they have in a grand child's life.

GRAND PARENTS

The love a grand parent is one of the most precious of all. Their patience, kindness and a willingness to sacrifice for the good of the family as a whole is something that can't be compared to anyone, but God.

FEARING HEARTBREAK

I walked all last night
I thought about what I'd say to you today
Hoping you had already forgiven me
For running away

I need to know that you're alright
I want to make sure you understand
I ran because I'm a coward
Afraid of a good man

Patience is of the essence
It won't be easy loving me
I'm not a stranger to heartbreak
Lasting love ain't never been for me

This brick wall standing here
Has been built for many reasons
I didn't appreciate the cost of love
Adopted bitterness in stormy seasons

Once again the appearance of love
Stands and stares me in my face
I tremble to think of moving this wall
For fear of another heartbreak

WIPE THE DUST OFF!

Wipe off the dust that's been gathering on your aching heart
Open the closet and let the skeletons fall free
Because even old bones deserve a brand new start
Unveil your face; show your true identity

The real you will attract real love
And you'll finally know the meaning of
What it is to live in your true destiny
And how to love yourself unselfishly

Wipe off the dust that's been gathering on your aching heart
There's a new day every twenty-four hours
Keep your head to the sky and keep God in your heart
And be a witness to His extraordinary powers

MY INDECISION

Broken hearted, and departed
Feeling crazy and retarded
Over rated, and over stated
Feeling highly aggravated
False conception, from major deception
Looking for a new direction
Recognition of my clouded vision
Represented by my indecision

My mental going on a warpath
My heart experiencing the aftermath
Inability to reach a sound decision
Example 2, of my clouded vision

Seeing, is actually believing it
Believing is actually receiving it
Mind lifted from this confusion
I'm letting go of false illusion
Not just concern about my vanity
Carried away from this insanity
Blocking out the sound effects
Regaining individual self-respect

Mindful thinking, not with heart
Holy Spirit, never depart
True God—true direction
True Love—true connection

MISSING IT ALL

Missing where we use to stand
Loving woman, romantic man
Characteristics of the perfect brand
Sparks had a visit from Mr. Sand Man

We're lacking that dramatic motivation
Bring back that charismatic flirtation
We need that systematic stimulation
My acrobatics greeting your rising inflation

Growing anticipation
High expectations
Pure intoxication
Steady rotation
Smooth circulation
No limitations
Heavy perspiration
Major hallucinations
Gasping notification
FINAL destination . . . .

Let's make preparation
For another presentation

FLIGHT OF THE CRAZY BONE

Feeling the bizzness of your shoe size
Power outage; got the body mesmerized
TKO'd by your special exercise
Can't stop the quiver of dancing thighs

Speaking in tongues unreal to me
Jumpn around like a damn chimpanzee
Running for the boarder like a refugee
Calling time-out like a referee
Back in the game by the count of three
Just can't stop, cause it so good to me
Greatest love and the greatest Kimestry
Don't stop now, keep serving queen bee

All this started at the collarbone
Working it down to the V-Zone
Ignoring the ring of the telephone
Nothing comes b4 that ice cream cone
Sending me to another time-zone
Watching me play your saxophone
Time to use the microphone
Now I'm playing your favorite song
In-yo-world; ain't NOTHING wrong
Amazing strokes of that King Kong
Invading my world with moans4 groans
Head first into the twight—light-zone
It's the flight of the crazy bone

TO BE CONTINUED—grinning

STARTED @ THE COLLARBONE—
(Grown Folks Only)

Phase 1

With that first kiss across my collarbone
Remarkable ability to quickly set the tone
Rain drops falling, pounding on the roof top
Thunder keeps calling to welcome Black Hawk
Breathing getting heavy; as intensity grows
Here comes the sunshine, followed by a rainbow

Phase 2

Totally mesmerized
Satisfaction multiplied
Perfectly harmonized
Beautifully sounding sighs
Personally gratified
No need to fantasize
Damn near hypnotized
Ready for lullabies

Sweetest piece I've ever known
Started at the collarbone

WHEN IT COMES TO YOU

I love the way you improvise
When your urgency is on the rise
Got a nack for dancing thighs
The truth is in your shoe size
It's beautiful when we harmonize
Relief that keeps us satisfied
Let me try to summarize
Why I've still got goo goo eyes

When It Comes To You
I have No self control,
Of my heart & soul
Can't seem to withhold
My Tootsie Roll
I quickly unfold
To welcome your gold
My remote control
Is on cruise control

When It Comes To You

I'm revitalized
Instantly energized
Your private enterprise
I'm your chinky eyes
You give me buttaflies
You more than tranquilize
You've got me hypnotized
I'm so damn mesmerized
With your special exercise
And extremely satisfied

(This is just a poem! Yall stop relating this stuff to me & JReed. We don't do this kind of stuff!)

INVITING YOU IN

I needed to invite you in
The urge to be close was more than I could bare
Any why'd you have to put your fingers thru my hair?
Touching the back of my neck with a glide, soft & smooth
Do you even realize you're doing what you do?
Hell yeah baby, I know you do

I pride myself on being a lady
But ladies need love too
I've never been known to move so fast
But my body started calling your name
And I knew you were getting this sweet potato pie

Damn, you smelled so good
And damn, I needed dat wood
So I led you to my bedroom
Damn, you're so damn fine
I felt your love rise & shine
So I thought I'd kiss your full moon

Your eyes just about rolled in the back of your head
So good you wanted to scream, but you stayed cool instead
Ten minute passed; you couldn't take it anymore
You unzipped my dress; watching it slide to the floor

Admiring the smoothness of my caramel skin
Black lace thong had you wanting to get in
Kissing my body from head to toe
Tasting my love like a motha frickin pro
Now ya had my eyes rolling in the back of my head
Explosion number one, then you put me on the bed

Discovering the tight squeeze, you didn't expect
It turned you on even more that it was also so wet
Tight, wet and warm, and the strokes began slow
TO BE CONTINUED. Ha ha.

HEATN' IT UP

Our heated tongues met at last
I've wondered if this day would come
Intoxicated with the thought of touching you,
Tasting too good to stop at just one
Craving every kiss you place on my collar bone
As the floor becomes our center stage
Sudden chills over-take me
As your fingers glide down my rib cage

My body suffers hunger for you,
Our clothes scattered across the floor
This tight squeeze seems to excite you
Makes you want me even more
Your slow motion and magnetic rhythm
Gives my love a moment to adjust
Arouses my flow to the max speed
As you pull out and switch to tougue-thrust

Warm, wet and perfect harmony
Tasting, teasing, and giving your all
The best of the best; this must be for me
That's your name I'm starting to call
My back is arched for you with the climax
As you threw me clear into ecstasy
You enter again and I'm filled completely
Your kisses tasting like sweet tea

The intensity grows as our fire is fueled
To demanding thrusts of passion
The sounds of love making fill this room
Moving towards stage two satisfaction
It's so good and I'm gasping for air now
Don't stop because you're taking me there
2nd sigh of climax relief, as I whisper your name
Letting you know that I'm glad you decided to share
It's my turn to take a ride now
While you enjoy the motion I bring
Lay back, relax and leave the rest to me
Let me show you how I work this thing

QUICKIE!

GROWN & SEXY ONLY
Candle waxing
Watching reactions

Purring kitten
Loving the slicking

Slobbin' the thobbin,"
Like Baskin Robbins

Moaning & groaning
Damn near foaming

Holding & squezzing,
Biting & screaming,

Heavy breathing,
Damn near wheezing,
F I N A L L Y . . . . RELIEVING

Never under estimate the awesome POWER of a quickie . . .

STAGE 1-2 3 XTAASY

Damn you got my heart skippin' major beats
Got me stuttering when I'm trying to speak
Been down town for damn near ten
Come on, I'm dying to have you in

Soaking wet and the rain wants to come
Loving the magic motion of your tongue
My urge is to pleasure your love orally
I'm pushing you back from tasting me

Gotta return whatcha been giving to me
Kandles bright enough for you to watch me
Telling me how damn good it feels
Trying to give me something I can feel

My body is calling and I can't fight it
Heart racing from the excitement
Loving the way you're grippin my hips
Preparing me for that powerful dip

Whispering how ya gonna take care of me
Looking forward to stage 3 ecstasy
Knowing you'll be too much for me
Loving the tight squeeze entering me

Ya bringing out the freak in me
Losing control & I'm grabbing the sheets
Scratches on yo back, tattoos from me
Don't stop what cha doing to me

Suddenly pulling out of me
Behind is where you're try to be
Gotta have you back inside me
Sliding in just a little bit easily

Moaning and breathing so heavily
Winding it up while ya talking to me
Knowing damn well you aint gotta ask
It's plain to see that you're waxn this azz

MY TRUE LOVE
Deep In Me—Like Poetry

My true love has my heart,
He knew it even before the words escaped my lips.
He be like poetry to me,
Deep in me,
Consuming me,
Assisting me in the creation of life.

My true love really knows me.
Like dis poetry,
He pushes that flow in me.
He waits for me,
He gravitates to me,
And just like dis poetry,
He satisfies me,
Never denies me,
He cries for me,
And longs for the love that's always like poetry,
To only come from me.

I BE WHAT HE NEEDS

I be that centerpiece,
That enhances his masterpiece.
I compliment and increase,
I be his elbow grease.
And when he needs to release,
I'ze be his one and only relief.

Ya see, I be his hydraulics,
My curves be so symbolic.
Working him like a workaholic,
Knock him out like sleepaholic
Like caramel and chocoholics,
He needs me like a foodaholic.

Yeah I be his honeycomb
Keeps him in that twilight zone
Takes him through that combat zone
Like the flight of the crazy-bone
Music is the moan & groan
When I satisfy the wishbone

REWIND

Let's rewind back to a time when our love was truly a love story
Let's rewind to the days when one another's needs were
mandatory
Promises were promises; no doubt if they'd be broken
When there was extra special caring in every word spoken

I hate it when we don't communicate the way we should
Tension rises when things we say are misunderstood
When things get rough, you seem a million miles away
Still, you have a gift for finding the perfect words to say

Let's rewind back to a time when kisses were like gumdrops
Let's rewind to the days when time would seem to stop
Let's go back and recap the moments of heated yesterdays
Let's stay home when it rains and discover new heated wayzzzzz
Let's lie around and watch movies, til one of us gets hungry
Let's take the phone of the hook, and play where we do laundry
Let's spin the cycle fast, and explode when it finally stops
Let's follow up that task, until our motors wanna pop
Let me hear you tell me over & over that I'm the best
Let's love each other more, instead of loving less

COMPLETE INTIMACY

Finally I've decided to follow my heart.
My life is my own to live,
And I intend to live it while loving you.

I look into your eyes to feel your spirit,
I touch your body to feel your soul,
I smell your scent to become aroused,
and lay down with you to experience intimacy.

I've come to grips with the simple fact,
That you are the blessing God has promised me.

You are my one and only love.
I am forever complete.

GIFT OF LOVE

I love you and I need you more than I can find the words to say.
Let's take special care of the love we've been blessed to know
Reminding one another of the times when our lives weren't so complicated
Renewing our passions and re-kindling the sparks that kept our relationship a blaze.
Let's always remember that love is so much more than candlelit dinners and slow jams . . .
It's full of patience and learning to forgive.
It's being supportive of each others dreams and understanding that at times we all fall short.
Let's never forget to laugh together when life is good and to share our tears when life seems wrong.
Let's remember that we are gifts from God to one another and that a gift from Him is a true treasure.

I love you

MY DEAR HUSBAND

You do so many things to make me happy
Things you may not even think I notice, but I do.
I need you to know that I appreciate all that you are,
And especially all that God is doing in you.

God must have known how much I would need you,
And I thank Him for the miracle of your life.
I praise Him for the love that last beyond the beginning,
And for the wonderful blessing of being you're wife.

I love you,
Wifey

I'M SORRY . . . AGAIN

I'd like to apologize for taking my frustrations out on you.
I want you to know that I realize how harsh my words can be.
Just because I'm having a difficult day doesn't give me the right to mistreat you
I hate it when there is any type of tension between us and I pray for the chance to make things right.
Your patience and forgiving spirit have been a blessing to me and the life of our relationship.
Your love and compassion are truly appreciated and I thank God that I am so blessed.

I love you and always will.

JUST U & ME

I love it when it's just you and me,
Laughing about all sorts of goofy things,
Sharing our most private thoughts,
Taking long walks together,
When all that matters in the world is you and I

I love watching you sleep.
I love hearing you laugh or even brushing your teeth.
I love our slow dances together when there's no music at all.
I love sharing our dreams no matter how big or small.
I think of so many yesterdays made wonderful by your smile,
And I look forward to discovering all the joys God will bring into our
future.

MY MAN, MY ROSE

Roses take on many forms
Today I noticed the rose in you
My husband, yes my one and only
Standing there, being the man you are
Head of our family, love of my life
Yet the heart and splendor of a rose
You should know how beautiful you are
And I wanted to be the one to tell you

LOVED AGAIN

Oh my love,
You saw me, as I was meant to be,
Not how I felt at the moment
Unselfishly you poured your love in
With you I've found reasons to love again,
You allowed me to cry the kind of tears,
That would release me from past pains and fears
I'm no longer afraid of just being me
I'm exactly as I should be
My life has been blessed with loving arms that hold me
Lovingly I shall hold you,
Until God decides to call me home

Signed,

Loved

LOVING THE PAIN AWAY

He loves her,
But she knows not how to love him in return.
She knows only what she's lost from giving all of herself to those who
were unworthy of it.

Yet he wants to love her passed her pain.
To restore what has been broken,
To prove himself not only worthy,
But to show her that the best is yet to come.

He wants to love her so that she never doubts,
How worthy she is of such an awesome love.

He is,
Her blessing,
From the One and Only True God.

RELATIONSHIP STUFF—
If you plan to reap it; sow it.

We often neglect the simple pleasures that use to bring out the best parts of our relationships. Re-kindle or keep the flavor by adding an unexpected, unanticipated, inviting pleasure to your regular daily routine.

Getting a babysitter for the kids and taking a 60-minute vacation in the master bedroom OR even in a hotel suite is known for charging the battery life of your relationship! It can make the difference between a routine week and a NOT-so routine week. Smile.

When we get in the habit of embracing our mates for no reason other then affirming your honey that you need to touch him/her, we open up a window of free flowing love. A little show of affection goes a long way.

Remember the art of complimenting your mate. It's always nice to know how irresistible we are.

Keeping a mental list of the qualities within your mate that sparked your interest when you first met is a must, especially in the times when they seem to pluck your nerves.

Taking a few of your mates responsibilities off of his/her plate gives them the opportunity to enjoy a hobby that they haven't had time for lately. This will prove to be a wonderful display of how much you care about them.

Never underestimate the power of a SLOW DANCE with your sweetie. (Nuff said.)

Never forget that uncontrollable laughter is one of the best bonding Experiences you'll ever have together. Some of the best memories come from a bunch of crazy laughter.

The power of a love letter can re-open a door within the heart when nothing else will.

If you plan to reap it; sow it.

WHO ARE YOU?
(Chant Rap for kids)

Question: Who are you?
Answer: I'm a child of the King

Question: What do you believe?
Answer: I believe in my dreams.

Question: And where are you at?
Answer: Where I'm suppose to be.

Question: And where is that?
Answer: Living in my destiny.

IT'S REALLY ME

This mirror stares me in the face
It's telling me a story I don't want to hear
Showing me what I'm almost afraid to see
It's forcing me to look deeper and truly find myself
To look beyond the cutie pie face & the chinky eyes
So there I stand
To my surprise
All grown up
My, my, my,
It's me

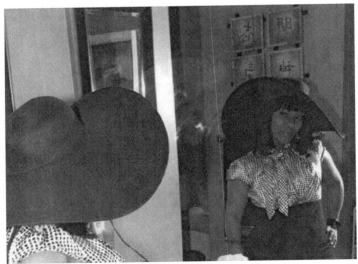

Photo by: Robin Brown /Titan Entertainment

WHAT IT MEANS TO ME

This poetry lives in me
Next to God and my family
There's only this poetry
Ya see, it's known me,
Since conception of me
So if your impression of me
Isn't what you think it should be
Then roll on by me,
Deny me,
It'd be fine with me
Cause you don't define me
I'm so blessed to be,
Apart of this poetry,
That fills me,
Send chills through me,
Even when I'm sleeping,
It keeps calling me
It shares my grief with me
Poetry believes in me
And when I want to explode,
It brings relief to me
It speaks to me
It teaches me
When my INK reloads,
Stories are told for me
Poetry's never old to me
Or ice cold to me
When my heart is aching
Poetry consoles me
It runs through my veins
And it flows with me
The grace of this Poetry
Has mad love for me
It keeps me alive
It gets me by
It understands my mind
It's my natural high
Nothing comes between my poetry & I
Cause It's from God

MY VOICE, MY PEN, MY CHOICE

As I allow
the swing of my pen
to lift and begin.
I could follow the trends
or dig deep within
and choose to praise HIM.

What I write is a choice
It's my right to rejoice
There's power in my voice
Bible ready for the hoist

I'm breaking the curse
New Life brings Re-birth
Changed my days on this earth
Now I know what I'm worth

NO LIMITS

No matter how big your dreams are; God's dreams for you will always be bigger. Putting a limit on your self is one thing, but putting limits on GOD . . . well that's just plain ol' stupid.

STOP HINDERING & START HELPING

When you repeatedly allow the same people to use you as a crutch & you repeatedly bail them out of their messes, you do them more harm than good. You are actually hindering their growth. It's kinda like taking medications that only bandage the symptoms instead of dealing with and eliminating the problem.

GET OVER IT

Stop trying to figure out why some people just don't like you!!!
There will never be a day when there won't be SOMEBODY that dislikes you. Not ever! So get over it. Allow it to motivate you to continue being that Fabulous Child of GOD you are!

GURL PLEASE

Stop making yourself believe that you are the ultimate sweetie!!
There are plenty of yousss out there! GOD did not start or stop making that good stuff with you!
Please believe me.

FALLING IN LOVE

Falling in love can prove to be so over-rated when all you get is the short end of the stick when it's over. Fall in love with being the best "you" that you can be & start making better choices. Love was not created to hurt people and it doesn't.

FINDING A GOOD MAN

So many people say that there is a man shortage, but I think not. There are plenty of men. There isn't even a shortage of wonderful men. They are all over the place! Instead of complaining about how hard it is to find one, maybe you should be a bit more selective. Try doing some research before you jump into a so-called "relationship with a man.

HATE EM!

I'm trying hard not to say I hate people, but I'd be lying if I said I like folks who talk about how spiritual they are, yet they aren't taking care of their kids There is nothing spiritual about being a deadbeat parent.

SLEEP WANTED

Stop trying to be a super hero! GOD made sleep for many reasons and "rest" is one of them. Get some shut-eye; the world will be here when you wake up.

TAKE CARE OF YOU

STOP trying to be everything to everybody!!!
Don't you realize that other folks have a survival instinct too?
Most of them will find their way, and if they don't . . .
It's not your fault. Do what you can, but take care of you too.

CHALLENGES

Every challenge you face is an invitation to a blessing. The sooner you start to see it that way, the quicker you'll try facing the challenge head-on & getting through it.

TRUST HIM

Remembering when I stopped trying to impress GOD and begin just trusting Him. Trying to impress GOD is plain ole "foolish." Trusting Him is the smartest move I've ever made. Be well

I'M WHAT GOD SAYS

There was a time in my life when I allowed the fear of failure to keep me from moving towards certain dreams & goals. Now I'm celebrating the attitude of HANDLING-my-Bizzzness . . . . even if I have to do it afraid and/or unsure of the outcome. The enemy does not have power over my dreams . . . God has already assured me of that.

JUST LISTEN

Conversation can be a positive thing, but only if what you're communicating means something to at least one of the people in it. There have been so many times I've been engaged in a conversation that never really caught my undivided attention, yet I decided to be polite & fake it through. But there is nothing wrong with just being there to listen. Sometimes that's all the help we need to be. It can mean more than you'll ever realize.

UGLY TRUTH OR PRETTY LIE

Excuse my expression—but the *ugly truth* is better than a *pretty* lie. Pretty lies are easy to tell, and the Ugly truth can seem as if it's more trouble than it's worth. But I'll take the ugly truth over a pretty lie any day. I'll take that "Ugly looking Truth" to the beauty salon & have it looking FANTASTIC in no time at all.

CHILE PLEASE

STOP thinking that you are THE ONE!!
Chile Please!
U just B the one for right now!
You don't have anything the other one doesn't have or can't get.

SEX & MONEY

When sex & money are two of the main issues that cause arguments between couples, you can be sure that things will get worse if there isn't some spiritual warfare going on. Prayer is the BEST weapon you'll ever have in that battle.

ENOUGH IS ENOUGH

When you've prayed about it & done all there is to do; sometimes you've gotta know when to let it go. There's no point in dragging out something that's gone kaput. If you've been with that person for 5, 10, or even 15 years & they still don't know if they wanna marry you . . . . something has gotta change.

HE'S NOT IN MY POCKET

Many of us would rather keep our faith in our back pocket instead of share it openly with others. There are folks that you'd never know were faith filled people if they didn't actually tell you. I'm not a perfect person, but I love GOD! You may catch me rolling my eyes, or falling short in some other way, but my LOVE won't change for GOD. I love HIM & I'm trying harder everyday to be better because of Him.

SAY IT TODAY

Death does not discriminate; it can come at any moment & people we love are suddenly gone. Then we are left with the regrets of not letting them know how much we love & appreciate them, which can be a heavy burden on your heart when you're hurting. Don't allow another moment to go by without letting others know how you feel. Ya never know . . .

SMART GIRL

I'd been writing NON-STOP for the last 4 days. While I'm loving the creative juices that are flowing like crazy, I sure am kinda tired. I told my 11 year old that I kinda wish someone would "turn down the voices in my head for a little while." She said "Momma, you'd go crazy without those voices because they are what you're writing about & you'd be REALLY crazy if you couldn't write" (Smart girl)

MEAN IT, OR DON'T SAY IT

There are at least 2 things that a woman wants to trust & believe you are telling the truth about when you say them to her. "You look younger then you are" and "I love you."

FAMILY & FRIENDS

SOUL MATE

My mother once told me, "Luck is when preparation meets opportunity." Twelve years ago one elevator ride changed my life. Although I was always mesmerized by the sway of your hips, your sexy smile and beautiful, chinky eyes, I never really knew the loving woman inside. A quick conversation in an elevator, led to hours of talking and I immediately knew that I had found my soul mate.

My love for you has grown into a bond that cannot be broken.
Your presence in my life motivates me to achieve greatness,
You've affirmed my belief that God answers my prayers.
You have become the blood that flows through my body.
Your touch melts my heart and your voice soothes my soul.
You are truly a blessing from God and I'm honored to call myself your husband.
You are my beautiful wife, my lover, and my best friend,
You're everything to me.
For the love that you give me, I dedicate my life to you.
Until I take my last breathe, I promise to love, cherish and protect you.
Some people might say I'm lucky to have you.
I say that God was preparing me for the opportunity to love you
And what God brings together, no man shall tear apart.

Love Always
J. Reed
Husband & best friend

BEAUTIFUL SIGHTS

I love the stars I see at night
I love the morning's day light
Nature is a beautiful thing
Don't destroy it, just go green

I walk by the lake day and night
I watch the sunset and it's a beautiful sight

Peace, joy and happiness is a wonderful thing
Keep a smile on your face so you won't look mean

Kimari Daniel Reed
My 11 year old daughter

TOP REASONS I LOVE MOMMY

I love you because you make the best TV dinners ever.
I love you because you say you love me all of the time.
I love you because you look younger than my friend's mom.
I love you because you teach me about Jesus and how to pray.
I love you because you buy me cool clothes and fruit role-ups.
I will love you even more if you could get me a puppy.
And I will love you the most when you clean up his poop so I won't
have to.

Jamie Madison Reed
My 7 year old daughter

SISTERS

A sister can be your best friend
Someone you can stand by through thick and thin
Someone you will support whether they lose or win
To love from the beginning until the end

A sister can still get on your nerves
She can make you sick with every other word
Someone who talks entirely way too much
Someone you'll want to tell to shut up

But I love my sister and I'm glad she's here
I will always love her more and more each year.

Kimari and Jamie
Sisters

BONDAGE FREE

"Don't fall for the prosperity of your bondage situation, it is only there to make you comfortable and complacent with the idea of being in bondage." it is not freedom, it only mimics freedom. Who the son sets free is free indeed! Freedom is real, be free!

Pastor Grant A. Thompson
Church of the Rock Praise Factory

WHAT'S LIFE

A single parent home?
Most of life with Ma and Pops,
Ending it upon sight of you and them together.
Yeah a family, being raised by mom, is that life?
Watching her work herself into an early grave, to give us life,
And the things she felt worthwhile.
No, not wants, but needs like love, respect,
Courage and responsibility.
She tried doing it all herself,
Too much struggle,
Too much pain from a childhood,
Filled with so many things,
That could go wrong and did!
We all go through right?
That's Life.

We all have a story to tell.
Ours in black America,
With unique overtones of chaos,
Bloodshed, addictions, suppressions,
Oppressions and regressions.
Too much for us to take in one sitting,
So we continue the cycle.
Hers and mine . . . ours,
Some oil to help relax you,
Takes the edge off a long day, so they say.
It took off much more than that for him and her . . . them.
And that's just the tip of this "Black Iceberg".
It's melting away,
Yet we find ourselves drowning in its freedom of expression
Away to obtain capital gains.
Looking back if you are fortunate,
Has anything really changed?
You still have wants
And Ma still is single
Trying to give supply your needs.
What's Life?

Kenneth Hill
cousin

TODAY, I CELEBRATE ME

For many years, I felt as though I had to accept the hand that life had dealt me and also the bad choices and decisions that I made in the process. Because of my own low self-esteem issues and lack of self-love I had become needy, took on other people's problems, baggage, and shortcomings as if they belonged to me. However, this kind of living and thinking was unhealthy, it was detrimental to my psyche, stymied my progress in life and continually caused me to perpetuate and display self-hatred and low self-esteem towards the most important person in the world—ME, MYSELF AND I.

I packed up all of the baggage of bondage that had held me captive for years. I packed up low self-esteem and self-hatred. I packed up all of my bad choices, bad decisions and mistakes. I packed up bad relationships. Yes, I packed them all up and did something that I finally needed to do once and for all—I forgave MYSELF. I forgave myself for believing and thinking that I was not worthy of love, happiness, greatness or the blessings that God said in His word are so rightfully mine. In exchange for my old baggage of bondage, I have a new found freedom—I CELEBRATE ME.

I celebrate ME because I am a designer's original! When God made me, he broke the mold! I am delicate, soft, bold, brassy, beautiful, special, silly, creative, enthusiastic, stern, compassionate, gracious, graceful, lady-like, phenomenal, loving, loyal, true and kind. I have curvy hips, full lips, short hair and milk chocolate brown skin. I am sassy and classy, ghetto and bourgeoisie.

I AM FEARFULLY AND WONDERFULLY MADE! I celebrate life! I celebrate love! I celebrate ME!

Minister Lisa Thompson
Church of the Rock Praise Factory

UNBORN

Lying on my back waiting to be pleased
He only thinks about his mortality
Something to live on after he's gone
Unaware that the gift he left me with, will be destroyed before long
Heart beating hard
Butterflies in my belly
Blocking him out, ignoring all the yelling
"Have it for me, I'll take care of you"
Said "Yes" a thousand times, but I knew it was something I wouldn't
dare do

Laying on my back
Waiting to be ripped apart
Wish I wouldn't have let him do it from the very start
In goes the vacuum
Out goes the jewel
"All done" says the doctor, as he looks at me like a fool

My head hung low
Three times is NOT a charm
"Step down" says the nurse as she takes me by the arm
I did it again
Can't look him in the eyes
I will be the only woman he ever will despise

Another chance is given
Delight to see the dawn
But so ashamed and broken
All my babies gone
Laying on my back
See the death angels wings
I hope God forgives me for all these horrible things
Unborn

Janique Nicole Evans
My 26 yr. old daughter
Norfolk State University—Class of 2009
Singer, Actress, Vocal Instructor
facebook.com/janique.evans

A FEW WORDS OF ADVICE

Life is a beautiful, joyous thing, so when you're finish with the upsets that you claim you can't do anything about, go on and live life. It's your decision. Decide to be happy!

Mrs. Janette Jacobs-Miller
Mom

YOU'VE NEVER HURT MY SOUL

We have shared many years
We have endured many tears
We have loved in and out of time
You've never hurt my soul.

My commitment to you has been tested
My love for you I've invested
We've laughed and cried
Babies were born . . . family has died
We have shouted and had silence
You've never hurt my soul

At times I feel incomplete as if a piece of me is missing
I know now why . . . . that piece of me is always with you to hold
You've never hurt my soul

I've questioned if this is where I should be . . . if you were the one for
me
I question myself no more
My heart is yours to hold . . . . reason being
You've never hurt my soul.

Sonya Patrice Pendleton
Sister

GOOFING OFF #1

Goose,
Moose,
Orange Juice.
(Snap fingers)

Jasmine C. Lee
My 22 yr. old daughter
Bowie State College Student

GOOFING OFF #2

House,
Mouse,
A couch slouch,
Hot, Pot
It all means a lot.
Not

Jheremy Thompson
My daughter's boyfriend
Praise Factory Drummer

NEVER 2 LATE

All this time I've been searching 4 my destiny
Running here & there, back & forth
Thru the galaxy
Sprinting like a pro, sweatin' cause it's hot
Got the right sneakers on
But I'm still in the same spot

I'm doing 2 much, I need 2 have a seat
He directs my path
His light is under my feet
Got my ears open and I'm ready 2 listen
What's next? What's the plan?
What's the goal? What's our mission?

Waiting 4 your orders, like a Navy Seal
Ready 2 attack with my sword & shield
This time I'm not afraid
Rising above the shade
Adjacent 2 the King, so my path is laid

"Girl please, you're over 40, u know it's 2 late"

"Sit down Satan! 40 is the new 30, I look 20; don't hate!"

The devil is a liar
Listen 2 him? NEVER!
I got my big girl panties on
I'm ready 4 whatever!
Time don't wait, but it's never 2 late
I have a purpose; time 2 let it come 2 the surface
Look out world, I'm bout 2 show u what I'm made of
LET'S GO!!!

Lisa Renee
Friend
Professional Actress
Createdlisa@yahoo.com

HE DID IT FOR ME—HE CAN DO IT FOR YOU

I was 15 years old when I noticed a small mass on the left side of my neck. Following numerous medical appointments I was finally informed that it was a malignant tumor, (Lymphoma), and surgery was recommended immediately. It was spreading rapidly & had the potential to spread across my entire face in approximately two to three months. It was estimated that I would have a short six months to live without radiation or chemotherapy. My mom started to cry and I just sat there in complete shock, I didn't shed one tear. The surgery was scheduled on February 21st. The week prior to the surgery I felt emotionless. It was as if I hadn't digested the situation and I was numb.

The surgeon informed me that I could possibly lose all feeling on one side of my face, the hearing in my left ear, and possibly look as if I'd had a stroke depending on how well my body healed. Finally emotions set in and I realized this was not a dream. I cried so hard before she took the bandages off. I was 16 years old and all I could think about was being afraid to die, and what I would look like for the remainder of my life. The bandages were removed and the operation was a success, but there was a 30% chance the cancer could return.

It's been nine years and I've been living a Cancer FREE life, with no radiation or chemotherapy, and no signs of it returning. Throughout this entire ordeal I remember my mom praying harder than I'd ever heard her pray before. If I hadn't believed in the power of prayer before, I sure do believe in it now. God's face has shined on me and I am forever grateful. For those of you who are faced with a similar struggle please remember that if HE did it for me; He can do it for you.

Keeni A. Henderson
Friend

HUMILITY KILLS B.U.G.S DEAD

Allow the power of humility to flow thru your life. It gives you a strong, peaceful inner strength. You will see people and the situation clearer. You don't have to always fight in order to win the battle.
Humility is a repellant for BUGS.
It kills . . .
Boastfulness,
Un-forgiveness,
Gossiping,
&
Strife
It kills B.U.G.S dead.

Thanks Kimmie for allowing me to share a small part in encouraging and empowering others in your book . . . I am humbly grateful . . . . I can not wait to see it hit The New York Best Sellers list.

Daijon Evans Wilburn
Cousin

The man who can find a virtuous woman has found a great thing. She is more precious than rubies, and more refined than all of time. When you're heart is heavy with burdens, she says the right things to keep you from hurting. When your so called friends fall by the waist side, she serves as your guide. When you need a helping hand, she's always there without a command. Need I say more?

Herb Austin

HEY PRECIOUS,

How are you doing? You were in my thoughts and prayers this morning. I wanted to tell you this so you can get ready. Your books/ writings will be a great success, in spite of delays or possible set backs. You will bless the nation with your God-given gift.

God Bless you.

Edna Marie Agurs-Hicks
Friend

Often times our hurt becomes our focus. Another might have been hurting inside and released it on you. Depending on that circumstance, try not to take everything in as painful intent and forgive even if you don't feel like it. Forgiveness is for you, not others.

Donna Burt Dantzler
Friend

God Power" the new hybrid <—trademark pending.

Steven Hill

FRIENDSHIPS

Friendship has always been something special in my life because as you get older you realize just how important having a friend truly is. So, I have written a few instances in my life where being a friend made all the difference in the world to me and sometimes it didn't. So here it goes.

Innocent Friendship—When we are young. It is the first "Best" friend you meet in grade school and all you do is laugh.
Chance Meeting Friendship—Being out with friends in a restaurant and you notice someone sitting alone at a table next to you but they are laughing at what you and your friends are laughing at too.
Family Friendship—Always there when you need them in good and bad times.
You being a Friend—You are there for them, but they are never there for you. You live and learn.
Work Friendship—It's your first day on a new job and you are scared. Then someone comes to you and introduces themselves to you . . . "Hi, I'm Kim and welcome." BOOM! FRIENDS OR LIFE.
Mother Daughter Friendship—It is a friendship that you develop over the years and the respect that you have for her because she is your mother.

I love you Kim and thank you for being my friend.

Yvetta Clark
Friend

THE CYCLE

I was lost and felt empty inside because of the way you treated me
I was lost and felt empty inside because of the dishonesty

We were suppose to be friends until the end but you tried to brake me
We were suppose to be friends until the end but you had a mask on so know one could see

Losing friends is not an easy thing to go through by your self
Losing friends will make you question your wealth

So you retreat and stay away for a while to gather your thoughts
So you retreat and stay away for a while to mend your broken heart

I was lost and felt empty inside because of you, now I have taken back my life and say no more
I was lost and felt empty inside because of you, now I am STRONGER then ever before

We was suppose to be friends until the end but I have moved on
We was suppose to be friends until the end but our friendship was torn

Losing friends is not an easy thing to go through because you can't fake it
Losing friends is not an easy thing to go through but you will make it

I was, I thought, I lost, and I am BLESSED to be here to be able to share this with you!

Sabrina Brown
Friend

PAY IT FORWARD

For years, I went through life wondering why I had to endure the childhood experiences that I had gone through. I wondered what good could come out of being raised in an abusive home while other family members enjoyed the benefits of two loving parents. For years, I wondered why I was the one who fought all through High School, constantly getting suspended and reprimanded. If not for the prayer of our mother and the mentors along the way, I don't know where I would be. All along, I only wanted to be loved, appreciated and understood. Over the years, the light was finally shed on my purpose in life. It all began to make sense years later when it was my turn to make a difference. I was asked if I wanted to assist an organization that specialized in mentoring young teenage girls. Suddenly, it became clear that my hardships would help some other young lady be granted a safer passage. That I could let them know that life doesn't end just because your parent(s) don't have faith in you. That even though you may seem like a wayward child, you need to recognize that to every cause, there is a reaction. All of a sudden it made sense, my role was to pay it forward and so I did.

Joy Pearson
Executive Director
Lend-a-Hand, Uplift-a-Child Foundation
joyp@lendahandusaVA.org

The primary goal of this organization is to develop Integrity, Vision and Authority in today's youth through mentoring and addressing issues they face on a day to day basis. These issues include bullying, social media skills, financial awareness, etiquette classes, peer pressure and more.

FROM ME TO YOU

Kimberley Evans-Reed,

You are a strong Black Tenacious God Fearing Woman. Your Character speaks for itself. Your class, positive energy, style, your grace, and definitely your swagger are at the top of the charts. You've touched so many lives in so many ways! You remain humble, witty, and funny but most of all you're grounded.

I met you when you were 16 and we learned we were cousins, and begin to build a bond that continued to grow over the years. God could not have placed a better person in my life.

Thank you for laughing with me, crying with me, keeping me encouraged when I needed, and thank you for the long talks and all the prayers. More importantly thank you for being you.

You know I know the lows as well as the highs and you are most deserving of the life you're living now! Words can't explain how proud I am of you, and the woman you've blossomed to be. You're my cousin, my friend but more importantly you're an inspiration to me!

I pray that God continues rain down so many blessings on you, that you won't have room enough to receive them all! But knowing you, you'll reorganize and find a place . . . even if it means passing those blessings on to someone else.
You're a Beautiful Woman of God, and His best is yet to come.

I can go on and on but I'll conclude by saying that I pray you'd continue to stay focused on your dreams of writing and putting into words what others may not be able to. Most of all continue to put God first in all that you do and always remember that I'm always on the sidelines cheering you on.

My, Cousin, my Friend, my Inspiration! I love you baby.

Love your cousin,

Bernadette Felton
Cousin

DARYLE'S RANDOM ADVICE FOR WOMEN

Please start being honest with your self about what's really going on with that man.
You need to love yourself more than you love him.
Stop ignoring the signs & his actions.
Respect yourself and other women.

WAKE UP!

He isn't really leaving his wife!
She most likely isn't as bad as he tells you she is.
He just tells you negative things about his wife just to get some sympathy sex from you & so you won't feel as guilty about sleeping with a married man.
And if she is really that bad, he should just leave her?
He isn't just staying with her because of the kids.

I'm a married man, & I'm telling you to STOP FALLING FOR THAT BULL!

Daryle Murrell
Friend

NEWNESS

What happened to the newness?
Where did it go?
Did you take it with when you decided to creep out?
Or did you take it while you were watching that screen?
You say it's not me, it's you.
So why don't you get yourself together?
The newness doesn't have to be only in the beginning.
Every day we are given new mercy.
Pay the newness forward.
Forget the fight, forget the lies, and forget the betrayal.
Yes, I know it's hard to embrace the newness the second time around,
but together we can do this.
Thank God for His Newness.

Altheia Lawyer
Friend

LOCKED DOWN

Up in the pen, lock down tight
Cruddy female, trying to get me life
Lied about her age, and got me caught in a cage
Trying to make it out of this concrete grave
Never really seen a joint quite like this
It's built to make you mad, and I'm always pissed
You better have the Lord, on your side
Or you might not make it out alive
Back at the county; bunk 18
I'm tierd of dudes whining about canteen
The over-crowded cells and the dirty azz bunks
The effin COs, trying to treat us like punks
Scared of ERT's because of what they'll do
Bum rushing in, to beat the hell outta you
Trying to call home - bottom lip split
Trying to figure out how to do their bit
People get extorted, robbed and beat
But all they wanna do is stay alive and eat
Stand up boy, and be a real man
And stop falling for that same wanna-be plan
Trying to get through this living hell
Baby momma just sent me some mail
I have one friend and you know who you are
We're gonna get-it-in at the CFE bar
For everything your've done - 'you're second to none
For all the fake azz friends, "Ya just lost one"
By now you should know how the saying goes
Ya always gonna reap exactly what you sow

Herb Austin
Friend

STILL STANDING

The year 2010 was one I will always remember because it the year my life changed as I knew it. I walked into my home and saw a note that said "here is your key". Immediate confusion came over me because I did not know what was happening. I walked into my bedroom looked into the closet and then understood what was happening. My husband of six years had left me. Over the next couple of weeks I experienced every emotion imaginable. It started with anger. How could he do this too me? Then I felt embarrassed of the entire situation. Along came bitterness because he was a coward who didn't deserve me anyway. Followed by revenge; I vowed to make sure he ended up right back where he was when I met him. Followed by panic; I began to feel afraid and wondered how I was going to maintain a household with now one salary. Suddenly I felt a sense of relief because I realized that this man was not an asset to my life, but a burden. The truth of my husband's character was undeniably in my face. Although I was hurting, there was a peace in knowing I was set free from future disappointment.

True healing begins with forgiveness. I knew that the only way to truly move on with my life would be to forgive him. Now all I feel for him is sadness because I know that we all reap what we sow and if you mistreat someone it will come back to you. He was not the man God had intended for me to spend the rest of my life with and I am grateful for this experience. When God removes the curse; He will bring a blessing. I am only being prepared for the true king that God has for me. And I will be his true queen.

I know that eventually God would bring someone wonderful into my life and I refused to carry any negativity into a new relationship. I have always trusted God and always asked for guidance when confronted with a situation. God showed me that I was stronger than I thought I was and that whatever I was going through would not defeat me. He also showed me that no matter how often the devil tries to knock me down, in the end I would still be standing strong. I learned not to allow anger, embarrassment, bitterness, revenge, panic or anything else cause me not to live my best life. You are stronger than you think. God will guide you. All you have to do is stand in faith and the Lord will see you through.

Carolyn King
Friend

LAST WORDS

As the time gets shorter, I can began to think about all the things that
can go wrong,
Not thinking of God's blessings that will keep me strong
And how He'll help me get through these hard and lonely times
Trying to keep positive thoughts on my mind
Not knowing what's out there for me to face
Feeling a little afraid to leave this place
Not knowing where I'm going or where I'll stay
I'm getting down on my knees to pray
Hoping God will get me through this day
I have no money or clothes to wear
I don't even have a change of underwear
I want to leave this place with my head held high
But I still feel as if I'm about to die
I'm taking one step at a time
Hoping I'll find some peace of mind
I don't want to give up on myself
Prayer is my one true wealth
I feel as if my back is up against the wall
Sometimes I don't like myself at all
I feel as if I'm beginning to fall
It's getting harder to stand tall
Feeling really sad inside
Feeling a huge loss of pride
As this cancer is eating me up inside
I want to go away somewhere and hide
God helps me stand by Him with pride
So I can smile even though I hurt inside.

William B. Evans III R.I.P. Daddy
6/26/49-8/12/2010

Me + daddy

-NIGHTMARE OF FEAR-

I wake up to a room so empty
Nothing left but me an the one you call "dark"
I hope for the light to spark; to show me where to start
It never comes! - Where to run; how do I hide
I hear noises yet nothing in sight
I begin to panic - I can't breathe - How could this be ?!
No walls in sight yet everywhere is a wrong turn
Independent by day - darkness hits an i need to know what's next
Where's the escape button from this chlostephobic cage
I'm desperate now to find the way
Screaming loud - no one to hear me - HELP! I need thee
Lonely; Confussed; afraid; - I kneel to my knees an pray
Please take me away I never wanna see this darkness again

Clorisa Curtis
Poet

The devil = ZERO

GOD = EVERYTHING!

Nuff said.

BUSINESS SECTION

Brother Reggie
www.rejoiceamericaradio.org
Roberta Elliott Speight
www.blogtalkradio.com/No-Turning-Back

Church of the Rock Praise Factory
Pastor Grant Thompson ♦ First Lady Margaret Thompson
Assistant Pastor Dexter Holmes ♦ Elder Juanita Holmes
1113 Easter Avenue
Capitol Heights, MD 20743

Mortgage Loans
James Reed/Senior Loan Officer
James.reed2@comcast.net
703-909-3305

Lend-a-Hand, Uplift-a-Child Foundation
Joy Pearson /Executive Director
Fredericksburg, Virginia
joyp@lendahandusaVA.org

Lamar Edward Exclusive Salon
Dervelle Harris/Celebrity Make-Up Stylist
Gerald Armstrong/Celebrity Hair Stylist
2127 Rhode Island Avenue, NE
Washington, DC 20018
www.lamaredwards.com
(202) 269 0958

From My Father's Kitchen Catering Service
Wendell Evans/Owner & Chef
Wendellev56@yahoo.com
www.frommyfatherskitchen.com
301-574-1098
240-304-2414 Cell

All "Ways" Cookin Catering
Waynette Lovelace/Owner & Chef
all_ways_cookin@yahoo.com
www.allwayscookin.com

Another Level Hair Studio & Barber Shop
Owners/ Ricardo & Yvonne Wanzer
728 N. Patrick Street
Alexandria, VA 22314
703-299-3063

The Twirl Factory Baton Twirling Team
Irene Johnson/Director
Alexandria Boy's & Girl's Club
Twirlfactory@gmail.com
www.thetwirlfactory.com
703-906-5361w

Chestnut's Tax Service
Edna Chestnut
301-967-1040 Office
301-967-1133 Home

Real Estate Appraisal Services
Carmen Hayes-Ruffin/Owner
www.kdaorders@aol.com
Audio Revolution Group/Senior Director
argrecord-onling.com

Ari's House of Dance & Performing Arts Studio, LLC
Rekisha Ari Squires
www.ahouseofdance.com
(540) 288-3888

Titan Entertainment
Keith Bell/Owner
Robin Brown/Event Coordinator
DJ's Photographers, Catering & Live Entertainers Services
www.titan-entertainment-djsuga.webs.com
571-235-6627

Revive Neuromuscular Aesthetic & Implant Dentistry
Revive Dr. Shila Yazdani & Dr. Michael M. Mortazie
3301 New Mexico Avenue N.W
Washington, DC 20016
202-363-3399

Home Improvement Services
Deacon Gregory D. Greene
240-354-1103

Total Experience Hair Salon
301-932-7880

Rachel Be Designs
Rachel Benson/Owner
the_original_dime_piece@yahoo.com

AGREEMENT—Musician/Band
Justin "J. Grant" Thompson/Visionary Leader/ Keyboards
ThePowerofAgreement@blogspot.com
agreement.music@gmail.com

Step 4 Band
stevethurman22@yahoo.com

Kush Boys Band/Jamal Weather/Mgmt
Members: Dread Tha Ol' Head, Baby Paw,
Brotha Rahim & Lucky Lamar
KushBoys.com

Spa Treasures, LLC
Ingrid Kindred/Owner
Natural and Organic Bath Products
www.spatreasuresonline.com

Labels Exchange
Monique Drummond
2417 B Mount Vernon Ave
Alexandria, VA 22301
703-836-2211

Another Level Hair Studio & Barber Shop
Owners/ Ricardo & Yvonne Wanzer
728 N. Patrick Street
Alexandria, VA 22314
703-299-3063

K Darien Appraisal Services
Carmen Hayes-Ruffin/Owner
Audio Revolution Group, Senior Director
ARGRECORDS-ONLINE.COM

TBS Facility Services Group, LLC
Tasha Berry
5625 Allentown Rd #107
Camp Springs Md 20746
info@tbsfacilityservices.com
www.tbsfacilityservices.com
877-8503827 Office
240-3516007 Cell

Capitol DC Photos
Hugo Rojas
Professional Photographers
www.capitoldcphotos.com
hrojas09@gmail.com
facebook.com/HugoRojasPhotography

CPSIA information can be obtained at www.ICGtesting.com
Printed in the USA
244276LV00002B/178/P

9 781463 433376